VOLVO 1800
The Complete Story

Other Titles in the Crowood AutoClassics Series

VOLVO 1800
The Complete Story

David G. Styles

First published in 2001 by
The Crowood Press Ltd
Ramsbury, Marlborough
Wiltshire SN8 2HR

www.crowood.com
This impression 2007

British Library Cataloguing in Publication Data
A catalogue record for this book is available from the British
Library.

ISBN 978 1 86126 195 3

Dedication
To my wife Ann, my daughter Emma and my son Philip, who
continue to endure long hours of desertion to a word processor,
or a library somewhere. Without the benefit of that indulgence
and support, I could not write.

Picture Credits
Illustrations for this book have been sourced from: Volvo Car
Corporation, Gothenburg; Volvo Car UK Limited, Volvo Cars of
North America Inc. the National Motor Museum at Beaulieu;
members of the Volvo Enthusiasts' Club; members of the Volvo
Owners' Club and the author. Road test data is reproduced by kind
permission of the editors of *Car and Driver*, *Road & Track*, *Sports
Car World* and *Autocar and Motor*, and drawings are reproduced
from parts and workshop manuals published by Volvo Car
Corporation.

Designed, edited and typeset by Focus Publishing,
11a St Botolph's Road, Sevenoaks, Kent, TN13 3AJ
Printed and bound in Great Britain by The Cromwell Press, Trowbridge, Wilts

Contents

Foreword

As a twenty-three year-old engineer and dedicated car enthusiast, I joined Volvo in 1969. The first car I was assigned to work with was the 1800. My dreams had come true and I thought I knew everything.

Now, more than thirty years later and as Senior Vice President of Research, Development and Purchasing at Volvo Car Corporation, I look back and realize how little I knew then, how much life can offer and that there are no limits for man or companies.

As a seed contains the DNA for a tree, and eventually a forest, Volvo in 1969 carried and cultivated the cornerstones on which the company has developed many generations of both cars and people. A heritage that has been the foundation of Volvo's success, the benchmark for competitors and the guiding principles for safety and environmental legislators. It was all there.

The sturdy and reliable 'drive it like you hate it' PV544 had been replaced by the 'family sports car', the Volvo 122, the new safe Volvo 144 had been introduced a few years earlier and the 1800 added emotions to to the core values of Quality, Safety and Reliability. These were no buzz words. They were, and still are today, the conviction on which we have built cars ever since.

Today, few things are the same. The car industry and Volvo have gone through a paramount change: new technology, new materials and new methods for engineering, testing and verification have replaced the way we worked then.

However, some things remain unchanged. My enthusiasm for cars and a belief that Volvo can continue its lead in building safer, better and nicer cars for families and individuals. We have accomplished a lot, but many things are still to be done and discovered.

Over the following pages there are many things to discover. Some of it I knew already because I was there. Some of it was new also to me. Therefore it brings me great pleasure to welcome you to join me on a trip through an interesting chapter in the Volvo history.

Hans Gustavsson,
Senior Vice President Research,
Development and Purchasing,
Volvo Car Corporation.

6

Introduction

Volvo is not a name instantly associated with sports cars. Indeed, exactly the opposite image comes to the minds of most people when mention of that name is made. One normally associates Volvo with solid, staid family cars that seem to last forever (certainly mine seems to be doing so). But then you have to consider what Volvos were doing in the sporting world some forty-odd years ago.

Volvo's first car was an open tourer, followed by a series of saloon cars. The first car to make its mark outside Sweden was the PV444, a car that would take on the best in rallying and often win. In the United States in particular, the PV444 was welcomed as an ugly bug (a bit like the VW Beetle) that was enormously reliable and took a lot of punishment.

When the PV444 had made its name, Volvo introduced the Sports engine and made a play for the sporty market. Then they produced the P1900, a glass-fibre-bodied two-seater, technically the equal of the Chevrolet Corvette, but a car which did not make a strong enough impression on the market, so was abandoned. But Volvo had now had a taste of the sports car world and wanted to create a flagship that would help to sell the broader Volvo image and products. So they embarked on Project 958, a two-plus-two coupé that would become the first truly internationally manufactured automobile, with parts sourced from both sides of the Atlantic and manufacture taking place in Sweden, Scotland and England.

Designed in Sweden and prototyped in Italy, the new car became the Volvo P1800. Its quality image, coupled with quite sharp styling for its time, almost guaranteed it

success and many a road tester has eulogized over this solid but very manageable little sports car.

Just when the 1800 was becoming a little tired, Volvo decided to take it one step further and create what one leading magazine branded a 'Sportwagon'. It was a name that stuck and the car was the 1800ES. Again, it did not sell in very large numbers, but it did make an impression and it did help to sell other Volvos. This is the story of the developments which led to the creation of the 1800 and its arrival in new markets; of how it took on the established sports car makers of Europe in distant markets and won its own slot in motoring history.

Many people have contributed to the creation of this book, so I hope that those who read it find it worthy of their interest. Allowing that many folk made contributions, I must name one whose efforts have been far beyond anything I or anyone else had a right to expect, but without his contribution, the book would never have made it to the presses. That man is Claes Rydholm in Volvo Car Corporation's Gothenburg Headquarters. Claes's work in the Corporate Communications Department was interrupted several times in my quest for illustrations, but he came up with what was needed every time. Most of the illustrations here are sourced from Volvo Car Corporation and the credit for securing them goes to Claes, though I must also thank the man who put me in contact with him, John Lefley of Volvo Cars GB Limited.

David G. Styles
Belton   2001

An interesting picture, this, in that the 'cowhorn' bumpers give it away as a Jensen-built car, yet the wheels suggest that it is an 1800S. In fact it is an early car, so is a West Bromwich produced vehicle, but with a variation on the wheels – perhaps already in plan, whether the car was to continue being built at Jensen's or in Gothenburg.

1   From Ball Bearings to Motor Cars

The Swedish bearing manufacturer Svenska Kullagerfabriken (SKF) was already one of the largest companies of its kind in Europe by the time our story begins. The company became popularly known as 'Skefko', and by the beginning of the Great War of 1914–1918, it was planning the establishment of a subsidiary to manufacture deep-groove ball bearings, which were named 'Volvo', from the Latin 'I roll'. By the end of 1918, the Volvo name had been shelved, as SKF had decided its own name should be used on all types of ball bearings produced in the group. In 1924, the name was dusted off by Assar Gabrielsson and Gustaf Larson, after they had agreed to join forces to manufacture cars. Their prototype appeared as the Model OV in 1926 and the foundation of one of Europe's largest industrial corporations was laid. The Volvo quickly developed into a solid, reliable car, but certainly no sports car – not yet, not quite!

Where it all began – a Volvo deep-groove bearing, showing the company name on the rim.

Assar Gabrielsson and Gustaf Larson in the early days of the company.

FROM LITTLE ACORNS

The two men who started the Volvo car business were from different backgrounds and had certainly set out to follow different paths in their careers. These two men were Assar Gabrielsson and Gustaf Larson. Gabrielsson was born in 1891, the son of an egg merchant in Korsberga. Larson was born in the year 1887 in Vintrosa, near Orebro, the son of a farmer. He became the engineer of this partnership, graduating from Orebro Technical Institute in 1911 and then developing his knowledge of motor vehicles in a post-graduate apprenticeship with White and Poppe in Coventry, the very heart of Britain's motor industry. Peter Poppe was a Norwegian and so the young Gustaf felt at home during his training there, since they shared a near-common language.

Gustaf Larson then returned to his homeland to continue his studies at the Royal Institute of Technology in Stockholm, from which he graduated in 1917, going on to work with SKF in Gothenburg. He left Skefko in 1920 to return to Stockholm and joined Nya AB Galco, a company that made sheet metal pressings and bearing materials. Larson was employed there as works manager and remained there until he was ready, with his future partner, Assar Gabrielsson, to launch the new Volvo car. Precisely how they came together is lost in history, but their formal partnership began with a verbal agreement to join forces, their specific objective being to manufacture in volume a truly Swedish car to take on the might of the imported vehicles of the time.

Assar Gabrielsson had planned for himself a business career after graduating from the Stockholm School of Economics. His father's egg importing business had bought most of its eggs from Russia, so young Assar had learned Russian and was to use it in his business dealings for SKF when he was appointed sales manager and travelled to Russia in the very early 1920s. Clearly, young Gabrielsson was considered very bright and possessed of considerable potential to have been elevated to sales management so early in his career. Further accelerated promotion was to come, as he became head of the company's French subsidiary. It was whilst in France that he became interested in the motor car and was convinced that there was room in the market for a new, all- Swedish car.

That there was considered to be the potential for a new, Swedish-built car was supported by the delegates at a conference of the Swedish Association of Engineers held at Stockholm in the autumn of 1925. The consensus of that meeting was that there was a need to bring together a team of men with the essential skills to manufacture vehicles and to raise the funding that was essential for the project to pro-

ceed. Larson was the man who could bring together the manufacturing skills, whilst Gabrielsson was the man who could almost certainly raise the finance. One potential source of funding was SKF itself. The two men had come together in the summer of 1924; they formed a formal partnership in December 1925 to build six prototypes of their new car, which would ultimately be called 'Volvo'.

BIRTH OF THE MODEL OV

Styling of the tourers was basically similar to the 1925 design of a body MasOlle had created for his own Voisin car. The nine tourers differed in detail from each other and all were painted in different colours to make them quickly identifiable. Whilst economy of cost had been a priority in the building of

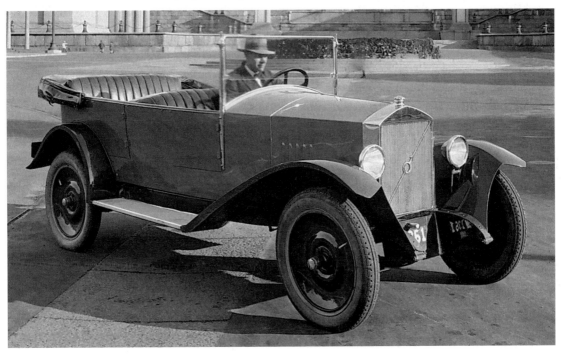

Helmer MasOlle's OV prototype.

these cars, the choice of Freyschuss was close to a guarantee that the new cars would be anything but cheap. At least, though, they represented a quality that would later become synonymous with the name 'Volvo'.

When it appeared, the car had a solid, even rugged, look to it, with its squarish lines, upright windscreen and quite Rolls-Royce-like radiator. There was no badge carrying the Volvo name on the front of the car, nor anything else visible from the outside that proclaimed this to be a Volvo product, for the name had not yet formally been adopted. However, that symbol which has become the hallmark of this Swedish vehicle, the old symbol for iron and, coincidentally, the symbol for the male of the human species, a circle with an arrow pointing upwards to the right at 45 degrees, did appear at the centre of a diagonal line from the bottom left to the top right of the radiator as you stood facing it.

The Pentaverken-built engines in these first cars were four-cylinder side-valve units of 1.9 litres displacement, fitted with a three-main-bearing crankshaft. The power output, according to the original 1927 brochure, was 29bhp at 2,000rpm.

The early Volvo radiator, showing the logo, which is the symbol for iron.

The low engine speed would no doubt contribute to the reliability and durability of that power unit, but its performance was certainly not earth-shattering, with a cruising speed of 37.5 mph (60km/h). On the other hand, Swedish roads at that time were not ideal for much higher speeds, as few had metalled surfaces. City streets were mostly paved, but rural byways were for the most part unmade tracks. The road wheels were of the metal disc type, fitted with 29 x 4.75 tyres, and Bosch six-volt electrics were fitted. The seats of the car were upholstered in leather and the fold-down hood was part of the specification. All in all, the new Larson car was a solid two- or four-door, four-seat tourer.

By May 1926, the secret was out, in that the press had learned of this new Swedish car being built by Gabrielsson and Larson. According to at least one report, it was said to be the product of the SKF Company, which, of course was not true. But, after a meeting with the board of directors of SKF in August 1926, Gabrielsson achieved several major steps forward in the prospective fortunes of his and his partner's new car manufacturing business. The first three prototypes of the new car, registered 'GL', were undergoing road trials as this momentous meeting took place and it was the confidence generated by those trials that persuaded SKF to invest SKr2,000,000 into the new business, as well as helping Gabrielsson to secure public funding support. SKF also agreed to release the company name 'Volvo' to the new venture, with Gabrielsson installed into the company as managing director with effect from 1 January 1927, Larson became the engineering and production director.

The factory of another ball-bearing manufacturer, Nordiska Kullagerfabriken, a company that had been absorbed into the SKF group some time earlier, was located in

The original Volvo factory at Hisingen.

Hisingen near Gothenburg. This factory was not in full-time use when Gabrielsson and Larson were looking for somewhere to manufacture cars and so it was handed over to them to be adapted to its new task. The three prototype cars currently under trial were driven to Gothenburg from Stockholm in the autumn of 1926, one by Gabrielsson, another by Larson and the third by Carlberg and Westerberg. No doubt, all of the documentation and records of the new company went with them in what has been described as quite an adventure, which it must have been, with no modern roads and a distance of over 200 road miles (320km). Work began on adapting the plant immediately, with the initial plan to commence production in January 1927.

It must be remembered at this point that Volvo was not the only Swedish car maker. Scania-Vabis was also active in the car market and, via its two antecedents, Scania of Malmo and Vabis of Sodertalje, had been making cars since 1903 (Gustaf Erikson had actually built his first car in 1898 in his Vagnafabriks works in the town where the Scania truck and bus plant is still based), as well as trucks from a very early date. The two companies had merged to become Scania-Vabis in 1911, and as time went on, it was decided that the truck business offered better profit potential than making cars. It was this move towards trucks that motivated Gabrielsson and Larson to move forward with their own car-making plans, though Scania-Vabis was still manufacturing cars and did not cease that activity until 1929. But the high level of foreign imports into Sweden, coupled with the high prices of Scania-Vabis vehicles, were two aspects of influence on Gabrielsson and Larson.

VOLVO COMES TO TOWN

Volvo's first brochure was published in February 1927, when it had already been decided that the original start date for production of the Model OV was to be delayed to April. This was largely down to delays in subcontracted supplies of components, although it also was partly due to the state of readiness of the factory at Hisingen and the need for redesign of certain components as the car slowly came to life.

17 April 1926 was a momentous day in the history of AB Volvo , for that was the day upon which the new Volvo car was revealed to the public and press alike. Similar in design to the prototypes, this was an orthodox-looking vehicle, with hints of American styling, but built with the stolid Swedish motorist in mind. It had to succeed, for a lot of SKF's money had been invested in it and high hopes were pinned on its success. The first car out of the factory gates was finished in dark blue with

Gustaf Larson

Lars and Hulda Larson lived on their small freehold farm in Vintrosa, near the town of Orebro. They named their third child Gustaf and he grew up on Falltorp Farm, taking a keen interest in sport and becoming a founder member of the Orebro Sportklubb, for which he played left winger in the club football team.

Gustaf Larson completed his higher school studies at the Orebro Technical Elementary Institute in 1911, going on to qualify as an engineer at the Royal Institute of Technology in Stockholm in 1917, after working for White and Poppe in Coventry, England, between 1911 and 1913. So well thought of was the young Gustaf's work, that one of his former professors asked him to donate to the Institute the drawings and calculations of his undergraduate thesis to be used as a model for students of the future. He went on to work for SKF in Gothenburg, where he met and worked with a young sales executive in that company named Assar Gabrielsson.

On Midsummer's Eve, 1924, Larson and Gabrielsson met again and had a brief conversation, a conversation which was to be the catalyst of a co-operation that led to the creation of the Volvo Car Company. Larson continued, for the time being, to work for GALCO, hiring others, including Henry Westerberg who was to be Volvo's first employee, to bring the first Volvo into being. From there, the company, and Larson, would never look back.

Larson was the man who originated the idea of producing the drawings and specifications for subcontractors to manufacture the Volvo's components. By this means, Larson calculated, he could have better quality control than by making everything in-house, because anything substandard could be returned to its maker for replacement at no extra cost to Volvo. Gustaf Larson reckoned that if he spent time ensuring quality of design, the finished product would not only be designed to a better standard, it would be made to a better standard, too. Volvo's reputation for quality quickly became a hallmark.

Larson held a firm grip of authority on the Technical Development Division of Volvo right up to his retirement in 1952 continuing as a Board member until 1958. Even after that, he remained a consultant to the company right up his death in July 1968. Gustaf Larson's legacy to the Volvo name was his obsession with quality and durability.

The early Gothenburg production line, showing cars being built in series (mass production does not seem quite the right word at this stage, though the company was clearly serious about producing cars in numbers).

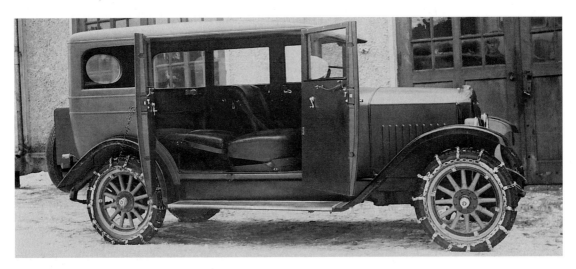

The Volvo PV4 Weymann Saloon. Note the pillarless design of the body and the fold-down seats, so if you broke down in Sweden's winter, you still had somewhere to sleep!

black wings. So was the second. In fact, this was the only colour scheme offered on those early cars – a bit like Henry Ford's philosophy of: 'You can have any colour you want, as long as it's black!' The logic was the same, too, for it eliminated the need to stock a variety of paint colours and made the whole finishing process easier.

This new entrant to the Swedish car market, then, was finally in production. The target was to build 1,000 cars, for those days a remarkable twenty a week. Of these, 500 were to be sedans and 500 were to be tourers; 40 per cent of the production total was to be exported. For a company with no track record in the Swedish car-making industry, an industry which itself had no track record in export, this was a pretty tall order and says much for Assar Gabrielsson's confidence in his partner's engineering skills and his own marketing ability.

The production Volvo was equipped with 20in wheels instead of the 21in of the prototypes, retaining the original four-cylinder engine (though it now had big-end journals of 55mm diameter instead of the original 40mm) and three-speed gearbox. There had been talk of a need for a six-cylinder engine, but the four remained, albeit slightly modified to improve bottom-end durability, as the power unit of Volvo's first car. Components came from various sources, the engines from Pentaverken, the electrics from Bosch (including a coil ignition system to replace the magneto of the prototypes), and drive couplings from Hardy in England, with the spiral gears of the differential also being British, made by Gleasons. The wheels were a concession to American taste, being of the wood-spoked, detachable-rim artillery type. And, at last, there was a badge placed on the radiator, with the word

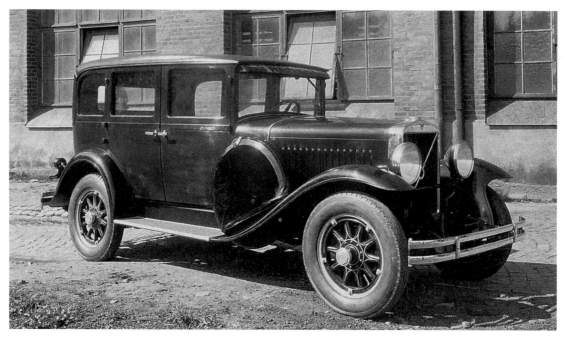

Volvo's PV651 Saloon, a big six-cylinder vehicle of robust and practical design.

*The Volvo PV652 Commercial Traveller, forerunner of the modern
Volvo Station Wagon.*

*The Volvo 650 Series was also available as public
utility vehicles, like this PV659 Ambulance.*

The PV36 Carioca was a very stylish car, which did not sell in great numbers, but heralded a significant step forward in Volvo styling.

The PV51 Saloon, not quite so stylish as the Carioca, but it sold in greater numbers.

'Volvo' in the letter style familiar to this day as the house style and with the words 'Gothenburg, Sweden' below it.

The first Volvo Saloon was the PV4, produced in the summer of 1927 as a Weymann fabric saloon type. To say it looked a little odd is something of an understatement, for the rear of the body seemed almost to overhang the chassis, and with the small box-type trunk stuck on the end, it looked quite ungainly. Fortunately, it did not last long as, by 1929, there was a completely new Volvo on the market, using the six-cylinder engine that had been suggested for the original OV series. The production forecast of 1926 had fallen hopelessly by the wayside, as only 200-odd open cars of the projected 500 were sold, although a modified saloon did sell rather better. Taking a leaf out of Scania's book, Volvo moved into manufacturing light trucks

as well. Even so, it was the middle of 1929 before the original 1,000 four-cylinder vehicles had been sold.

NEW CAR – NEW ERA

After a year of trials, Volvo's new car, the PV651, was announced almost exactly two years after the OV4 had been launched from Hisingen. The PV650 was produced as a chassis-only for coachbuilders. The identification characters were: 'PV' for Private Car, '6' for a six-cylinder engine, '5' for the number of places in the car and '1' for the body type or '0' for no body. Then there was the taxi chassis, identified as 'TRL671', a seven-place vehicle. There was even a sedan type with a full-height hinged rear door, built especially for commercial travellers (as field salesmen were called then). This version had removable rear seats to

---

Helmer MasOlle

Helmer MasOlle was born in 1884 in the Dalecarlia province of central Sweden. Art was his passion and as he grew up, his work became well known in his home province, then spread across Sweden. He became internationally known as a painter of landscapes and portraits.

Another interest of Helmer MasOlle was cars. He owned an early Voisin Tourer which he had re-bodied to his own design in 1925 (it has been suggested it was a 1914 chassis, but that's not possible, as Gabriel Voisin did not start manufacturing cars until after World War I). The original car had a torpedo body, which MasOlle replaced with a flat-sided tourer, retaining the original mudwings, fitting front and rear seat windscreens and front-hinged doors. The car featured in the Swedish motoring magazine *Svensk Motor Tidning* in the summer of 1925 and came to the notice of Assar Gabrielsson and Gustaf Larson.

Since the Volvo founders were looking for a designer for their first car, it seemed entirely appropriate to talk to Helmer MasOlle, who had a relative working for SKF and so could be easily contacted. Many years later, the artist declined all credit for the saloon version of the Volvo, which had a distinctly French look about it, but somehow did not have the elegance and balance of his tourer designs. This was the eighth prototype and it is pretty clear that, since MasOlle designed all the others, all of which differed from each other in minor ways, he was also responsible for this one. But, like most artists, if a work fails to come up the originator's expectations, it's probably easier to disown it!

MasOlle was commissioned to do other design work for Volvo, but will always be best remembered for his work on the Model OV. While he remained interested in cars, he returned to art as his prime source of earnings, painting many portraits. He died in 1969.

allow an increase in stowage space. Thus, the station wagon was far from a new idea.

By the 1930s, more variations on the 650 chassis were being offered. There were utility vehicles, such as ambulances and hearses built on the 650 chassis, as well as a cabriolet. Coachbuilders were producing examples of their art on Volvo chassis, too, so the name was becoming established and, much more to the point for Assar Gabrielsson, profitable. Jarbo built a coupé on a 650 chassis which was very reminiscent of the American types of the day, whilst a Kellner design was used as the basis for the Volvo cabriolet, which resulted in a car that had more than a passing resemblance to the Packards of the day. As 1933 drew to a close, so the 652 was eclipsed by the 653 and 654 models for the 1934 season.

The American styling influence continued to be present in Volvo design. Now, wire stud-mounted wheels were used, though the taxi-cab and some coach-built

examples used disc or artillery-style steel wheels. Norrmalm of Stockholm was one of those coachbuilders that went to work on the Volvo chassis with particularly pleasing effect. It seems that only one example of the Norrmalm cabriolet survives, but it is an especially elegant and sporty looking car. The next model in the line, the PV658 and 659, was the last of the 'upright' Volvos, as design was progressing at an almost alarming rate, with Riley in Great Britain coming up with its 'airline' styling, as demonstrated by the Kestrel Saloon, and Chrysler in the United States announcing the 'Airflow' sedan, both in 1934.

Volvo's response to the British and American aerodynamic styling was its PV36 'Carioca', designed under the supervision of Ivan Ornberg, a Swedish emigrant who returned from the United States in 1933 to take over the management of Volvo's car division. In the process of

The PV54 took on much more of the American style of the period. This one has been adapted to operate on self-generated gas for use during the war years. The camouflage tells us it was a military vehicle.

Assar Gabrielsson

Assar Gabrielsson was born on 13 August 1891, the eldest of three children. At the time Assar was born, his father worked in the offices of Korsberga Brickworks, but Gabrielsson senior decided he could better provide for his family by running his own business. As a result, he rented farmland on the Spanafella Estate in Tibro, where he started an egg business that grew into a major importer, even bringing eggs into the country from Russia.

The family moved to Stockholm as young Assar's education progressed and he attended the Norra Latin High School, moving on to the Stockholm School of Economics, where he graduated with distinction. Fluent in Russian and English, Gabrielsson was employed in the Swedish Parliament for a few years as a stenographer, working also for his father's business as time permitted. In 1916, however, he decided he needed career growth and went to work for SKF in Gothenburg. By 1921, he had been appointed managing director of SKF France, but just over a year later was back at Gothenburg, appointed Group Head of Sales. It was Gabrielsson who negotiated with the Russian Revolutionary Council over the confiscation of the SKF plant in Russia.

Initially meeting Gustaf Larson between 1917 and 1920 on a number of SKF company projects, Gabrielsson was impressed with the engineering prowess of the man who was ultimately to become his partner, though he had no inkling yet of that partnership. It was in 1924, when they met by chance in Stockholm and formed the partnership to make a Swedish car, that both realized a common ambition and established in the process a company that was to become one of the world's leading industrial corporations.

It was Gabrielsson who persuaded SKF to allow both the Volvo name and the dormant company bearing that name to be revived as a car maker. And it was he who persuaded the company to invest SKr 2,000,000 in the revived Volvo business. During this time, the ten Volvo prototypes were under construction, and three became ready for a gruelling test. That test was a drive from Stockholm to Gothenburg on unmade roads, after which the company moved into the SKF factory on Hisingen island.

On 14 April 1927, the first production Volvo car left the Hisingen factory under the supervision of Assar Gabrielsson, who remained managing director of the company until his retirement in 1956, becoming Chairman of the Board until 1962, the year in which he died. He had supervised the creation of the cornerstone of Sweden's motor industry. What was more, he had nursed the company through the depressed 1930s, guided its destiny through the difficult years of World War II and approved the export of Volvo cars to the United States. Assar Gabrielsson had left his indelible mark on the automotive industry of Sweden and Europe.

creating this new and radical departure from Volvo orthodoxy, he barred either Assar Gabrielsson or Gustaf Larson from seeing the design until it was in wooden 'buck' form. This new car took the Swedish market by storm and, considering how few were actually built (only 500), it found its way into some pretty far-flung locations, including South America, from where the name had come.

With only 500 Cariocas being built, Volvo had to produce something to earn its income, so the 650 variants continued in production until 1937. But by 1936, a development of the PV36 had appeared, abandoning the independent front suspen-

*The Volvo PV801 was the largest car in the range before World War II
and was a far cry from sporting vehicles, thus typifying Volvo's
wide scope in design and manufacture.*

sion as too high a production cost, because Volvo was now seriously looking at the market being taken in Sweden by Opel, Ford and others. So the next car in the Volvo line-up was the PV51, whic retained much of the styling of the PV36, as well as the 3.7 litre six-cylinder power unit. Still not built in unitary construction, the PV51 was a slightly simplified styling exercise, aimed at economic production and so equipped in quite spartan fashion. For example, only one door had an armrest, the seating and door trims were in an inexpensive cloth and only one windscreen wiper was fitted to the now flat one-piece screen.

The body of the PV51 was constructed from all-steel-sheet pressings, but still on a cruciform chassis, so that bodyless chassis could still be sold to coachbuilders – and a surprising 205 were sold as chassis, some having utility bodywork, others being cabriolets. In June 1937, the twenty-five thousandth Volvo rolled off the line,

and the company had now become a public company, SKF having released its shareholding to the stock exchange a couple of years earlier. The PV52 was essentially the PV51, but substantially improved inside. Special models were built with extended luggage compartments and Nordbergs built a number of cabriolets which were very reminiscent of contemporary BMWs.

The PV53 and PV54 continued the Volvo line started by the PV36, whilst the taxi cab market was now to be provided with something much more American in style, the PV801 and PV802 (the '2' denoted there was no glass division between driver and passengers), a big Buick-like eight-seater, revealed to the market in 1938. A similar design, the PV60, was announced in 1939 to replace the earlier '50' series of cars, but did not reach series production until after World War II had ended. The PV53 to PV57 models and the 800 series models were produced in some numbers during the war, but material supplies and wartime austerity even affected Sweden, despite its remaining a neutral country throughout the conflict (other countries in Europe were manufacturing the tools of war and so supplies of materials and components were restricted).

VOLVO'S QUANTUM LEAP

Whilst Sweden was not involved in World War II as a participant, it was not able to remain entirely aloof from that conflict, not least because the German war machine wanted to get to Norway so as, it thought, to 'pincer' Britain. The only way to Norway was through Sweden and, whilst the transient Germans did not intrude on Sweden's

neutrality, it became pretty obvious to most thinking Swedes that they would face a more austere future after hostilities ended, whoever would win. As a consequence of this realization, Volvo began to look more closely at the prospect of creating and manufacturing a smaller car.

A fellow called Helmer Petterson was brought in as a consultant to the Volvo design team. He had worked in the 1920s with the Excelsior Motor Company in the United States, one of America's most innovative motorcycle makers before it succumbed to Indian, and had returned to Sweden in the 1930s, working for a seqquence of Ford and GM dealers. Petterson was keen to produce a smaller car than was now typical of Volvo, as he felt the post-war market would demand more economical transport and, besides

The Volvo factory in 1941 (approx.); note the number of truck chassis around the yard

The prototype Volvo PV444 – the first of a completely new generation of Volvos.

that, it would give Volvo a better export potential, because virtually all the countries to which it visualized exporting were participants in the conflict. Petterson estimated that all the post-war European economies would see higher taxes on fuel and a general level of austerity that would last for some years after the war had ended. He was, as history has recounted, entirely right.

Petterson's first thoughts gravitated towards front-wheel drive as the means of propelling this smaller car. His second thoughts led him to believe that a two-door, four seater was his goal. A lot of ideas were put on to paper and after many early discussions he believed his idea of front-wheel drive would be accepted. However, when the car began to take shape on the drawing board, Gustaf Larson vetoed the idea of front-wheel drive on the grounds of production cost, which would have a serious

effect on pricing, and maintenance costs, as a front-wheel drive would be less accessible to work on, and so more costly to maintain. There was, it seems, a certain rivalry between Gabrielsson and Larson over the people each employed, such that if one of them employed someone new, the other would often think ill of the appointment, and thus the appointee. So Petterson decided not to rock the boat and settled for rear-wheel drive.

Despite war raging all around them, the Volvo team had set a target announcement time for the new model of autumn 1944, but design ideas were still being tossed around as late as the summer of 1943, which did not leave much time to create the new car and put tooling for its manufacture in progress. Larson was very interested in keeping abreast of developments as this new model came closer and closer to production. Various design teams were given segments of the car to develop under the overall supervision of Erik Jern, who retained a strong influence over the development of the engine. A fellow named Stig Hallgren had responsibility for the transmission, whilst Sven Viberg headed the development of the systems. Edward Lindberg, a former Studebaker man, took charge of body design, and the car, the new PV444, slowly progressed towards that 1944 release date. Bearing much of an American line to it, the PV444 was quite a shapely car for its day and, with relatively simple mechanicals, it promised to be as good a seller as anything Volvo had built hitherto.

2   After the Conflict – The PV444 and Beyond

In 1943, Volvo was ready to launch itself into an entirely new product range and a new manufacturing technique. In preparation for the new product, the PV444, and for the new tooling which it would have to acquire to make this new and adventurous model, the company had increased its share capital on the Stockholm Stock Exchange to twenty-five million Kronor. Whilst this was clearly a fund-raising exercise for the company, it was also an opportunity for existing and would-be shareholders to express a vote of confidence in Volvo. That they expressed that vote of confidence is a matter of record, as it is that the funding was made available.

The decision to manufacture a car of unitary body construction was not just a new venture for Volvo, it was a major philosophy change that had yet to be sold to the Swedish motoring public. The Swedes have a reputation for being conservative in their buying tastes and to think of buying a car of a type of construction that was, as far as they were concerned, unproven in their country, demanded a very major level of confidence in the designers and assembly crews. Much of the process of gaining that confidence was clearly down to marketing, but the design of the body line was also a very important ingredient. The body line of the finished product, according to Helmer Petterson, was based quite closely on the lines of Pontiac and Ford, so because the car would *look* right, it was thought that people would decide it was right, and go out there to buy it.

SETTING THE TREND

Design engineering on the new PV444 was running at a high pace by the summer of 1943, for now it had just a year in which to be completed in order to meet the planned launch, scheduled for September 1944 at the Royal Lawn Tennis Hall in Stockholm. But, before that, there was a lot of time to be spent on drawing boards and calculations, as well as a lot of development work to be done. The design philosophy had begun with the view that after the war, a smaller car would be more desirable than the current-sized Volvos, and so it was important to the company's future to be there at the forefront of the market. The Volvo team knew that the rest of Europe's industry after the end of the war would have major industrial repairs to undertake before production of anything could recommence. This would give Volvo a potential headstart, with a chance to build a healthy home market with virtually no competition, as well as the opportunity to exploit exports.

A team of forty people undertook the design and development of the new car. Gustaf Larson kept a careful eye on progress and would periodically offer a viewpoint, which would rarely be ignored. Helmer Petterson's original idea had been to go for a front-wheel drive car, using a horizontal four-cylinder engine of just under 1·5 litres capacity. Key features of

The PV444 at its launch in the Royal Lawn Tennis Hall, Stockholm.

this engine were to be ease of access to the carburettor, which would have been positioned at the front of the engine compartment, and to the distributor, which would be positioned vertically towards the rear of the engine compartment, being driven off the crankshaft. The spark plugs were vulnerable, though, as they sat horizontally at the front, so weather shielding was going to be necessary, especially taking into account Swedish winter weather conditions.

A wooden mock-up of the engine was built to consider its layout, the positioning of ancillaries and the mountings, combined with gearbox and drive couplings. This proved to be a waste of time

and design energy, because Larson ruled it out on the grounds of production costing, to say nothing of market acceptance. He believed that the traditional Volvo buyer would expect a more conventional layout, so he ruled that the new car was to have an in-line four-cylinder engine, with an orthodox gearbox and rear-wheel drive. The focus of attention would now return to the task of designing a unitary body.

In order to study more closely the characteristics of a unitary car body, Volvo acquired a 1939 Hanomag to establish how that company had addressed the problems of eliminating a conventional

The PV40 Saloon would have been a most interesting car, but it did not reach production. This is a full-scale mock-up.

chassis in its design. A number of ideas were taken from that vehicle, while others were the result of Peterson's team's own calculations. The body styling had to be up to date without being too adventurous and, of course, the best of current America styling had to be taken into account as guidance.

One of the first small car designs to be modelled in full size was the Type PV40. This was a highly adventurous creation which had been designed with a rear-mounted, eight-cylinder two-stroke engine by Olle Schjolin, who had returned to Sweden from the United States, where he had worked with General Motors. However, while it was well-proportioned, it was felt that its styling was slightly too American, as well as seeming to lose the sense of Volvo's character. Also, for the same reason as Petterson's front-wheel drive car was stillborn, this model was considered likely to cost too much in production tooling and

to be too unorthodox for contemporary Swedish tastes. Interestingly, Professor Porsche had already created his People's Car in Germany, and its military counterpart, the Kubelwagen, was proving its worth on the battlefields of Europe and North Africa, so the rear-engined concept could have worked. However, it was not for Assar Gabrielsson or Gustaf Larson, so work continued apace on a more orthodox Volvo for the future.

A full-scale model was built of the PV444, once the lines and most of the detail had been resolved, and was taken out of the factory for Gabrielsson and Larson to examine, so that they would see it in as near a natural environment as possible, rather than judging it in the clinical atmosphere of a design studio. The car was approved and build of the first three prototypes began with all speed in 1944. The exhibition at the Royal Lawn Tennis Hall was now looming large and so a major con-

The PV444 engine in the prototype.

centration of effort was required to get one car finished to an exhibitable state, to say nothing of the pressure on the suppliers of components. Even though the car was not actually able to be driven, the first prototype appeared on time in Stockholm and received a tremendous accolade from press and trade alike.

So impressed were the two principal directors of the company with the result of Petterson's teamwork, that they insisted that all the employees of the company should also see the car, to express their reaction to Volvo's 'People's Car'. Two trains were laid on to take employees to Stockholm for their own special viewing of the car which was to make their future. That was no mean feat, considering that Sweden was surrounded by the events of World War II. Almost 150,000 people visited the exhibition at the Royal Lawn Tennis Hall and Volvo used the entry ticket numbers to run a raffle, the prize from which was a new Volvo PV444. The exhibition actually featured the whole range of Volvo products of the time – cars, trucks, agricultural tractors and even military vehicles (Volvo wanted to show the people of Sweden that it was able to meet the country's defence needs if it should be necessary), as well as marine and aviation equipment.

INTO PRODUCTION WITH THE PV444

There seems to be some confusion in history about how the Swedish 'People's Car' acquired its designation. One suggestion is that it had four wheels and was announced to the public in 1944, though the more likely theory is that it was a four-seater with a four-cylinder engine producing 40bhp. Whatever the theories, this new four-seat-

ed two-door car was intended to go into production in early 1945, but the workers of Sweden had other ideas, for February 1945 saw the start of a long national strike which brought the whole of Swedish industry to a standstill well into the summer of that year.

The first consequence of that strike upon Volvo was that its headstart in the post-war car market was frustrated, because the 444 did not reach volume production until 1946, by which time other new designs in Europe had been released to a curious, if not particularly cash-rich, market. For example, Riley, in Great Britain, announced details of its all-new post-war 1·5-litre model in the first week of August 1945, just days before the first atom bomb was dropped on Hiroshima. However, while the Volvo PV444 had a cosmopolitan air about it, Riley's new car was distinctly British and distinctly more expensive than the Volvo. Even though there was a year's delay in the 444's production, its price had been set in 1945. Amazingly, that price was exactly the same as the price of the original Volvo OV4, released eighteen years before! The price was SKr4,080. How's that for inflation control?

Whilst the strike was causing horrifying problems to the production schedule, Volvo was not wasting time, for a prototype was touring the country, being displayed at dealer premises all over Sweden. People had to be kept aware of progress with the new Volvo and the 2,300 customers who had placed advance orders back in September 1944 had to be kept faith with. The prototype had to be demonstrated to all seventy-six Volvo dealers from Malmo in the south to Kiruna in the north. Members of the public turned out to see the new car in their droves and so the mould for Sweden's 'People's Car' was cast. A further proving

Early production PV444s on the production line; compare this with
the earlier picture of the OV4 in production in the 1920s.

of the car was undertaken when Helmer Petterson took a PV444 on a 838-mile (1,348 km) high-speed trial over unmade roads in a single day, averaging almost 28mpg (7·9/100km), which may not seem too startling for a 1,400cc engine, until you realize that the average speed over the run was over 60mph (97km/h) and the conditions were certainly not their best.

In order to get the car into serious production, Gabrielsson despatched his chief car designer, Carl Lindblom, to the United States to try to persuade the US steel makers to supply Volvo with sufficient steel to get the car into production, so enabling the Swedish steel industry itself to build up to a viable level in the meantime. The prototype PV444 was

repainted in a pale green and shipped to the US in the hope that it would stir the American steel giants to soften and give Volvo the boost it needed. But it was no go. Wherever Lindblom went, America's steel companies all came back with the same answer. They needed all their reserves to supply the huge post-war demand being placed upon them by the US car makers. The only beneficial result of Lindblom's US tour was that he was offered a job there which, after completing his specific mission for Volvo, he accepted.

The only benefit that Volvo drew from the delay in producing the new car was the opportunity to take stock of the design and the accessories used, and to make a few

LEFT: *On their way to the United States of America – a large batch of early PV444s.*

RIGHT: *Once in America, the Volvo PV444 quickly established a reputation for itself as a tough little car and as a sporting event winner. This ad tells of Volvo success in the Lime Rock Little Le Mans race – first, second and third.*

BELOW: *The PV444D at a typical Swedish weekend retreat in the middle 1950s, complete with family.*

VOLVO
wins
again

SWEEPS
FIRST THREE PLACES
IN 10 HOUR
ENDURANCE RACE

Volvo, the sensational Swedish-built family sports car, has added another win to its ever growing list of conquests in the world's toughest auto competitions.

Volvo's latest victory came Saturday, August 2, with the running in Lime Rock, Connecticut, of the Little Le Mans endurance race for imported sedans. Just as they did last year, the Volvo entries swept the field 1-2-3, further establishing Volvo as the performance and endurance leader among imported family cars.

Here is additional proof that no matter what the contest—speed, endurance, or economy—Volvo is a consistent winner. Already this year Volvo led its class in the arduous Pikes Peak hill climb in Colorado, won the gruelling Monte Carlo Alpine Run, the nerve wracking 2,000 mile Tulip Rally in Holland, the Swedish Mobilgas Economy Run, and famous Royal Swedish Auto Club "Race to the Midnight Sun."

Drive Volvo, compare it with any car in its price range, and you'll see why they say "One Try—and You'll Buy."

Volvo Distributing, Inc., 452 Hudson Terrace, Englewood Cliffs, New Jersey • Swedish Motor Import, Inc., 1901 Milam St., Houston 2, Texas
Auto Imports, Inc., 13517 Ventura Blvd., Sherman Oaks, Calif.
In Canada: Auto Imports (Swedish) Ltd., 459 Eastern Ave., Toronto 8 • 1350 E. Georgia St., Vancouver 6

changes. Even though no 444s were manu-factured before 1947, Volvo's profits had risen to a record level, with a 93-million Kronor turnover. This was entirely down to the growth in the company's truck, bus and tractor production, as well as its con-tribution to the country's military vehicle and equipment inventory. But, by 1947, Volvo PV444s began to appear on the streets of Sweden, all finished in Henry Ford's favourite colour – black! That was simply because the pigments for other colours were not yet freely available in a world recovering from the ravages of World War II. Despite this very long gesta-tion period for the 444, over 10,000 of the 12,000 cars placed into the production schedule by February 1947 had been pre-sold, though the price had risen to SKr6,080 by the time the car actually started to roll out of the factory in any numbers. Even this price was not going to make a substantial profit, but Gabrielsson felt he had to keep faith with those 2,800 people who had placed orders back in September 1944, and so he held the price of their cars to SKr4,800, the original fig-ure quoted when the car was announced.

MOVING TOWARDS A SPORTING HERITAGE

By the end of 1948, the Volvo PV444 was in serious production, though perhaps not yet volume production, with just under 3,000 cars leaving Hisingen by the year end. However, within twelve months, car pro-duction figures exceeded those of trucks and buses, and by the autumn of 1949, a limited edition of 700 cars was announced, to be called the PV444 Special (PV444S). No mechanical changes were embodied in this special edition, but it was a foretaste of what was to come – and, particularly, it

broke the mould. Volvos were no longer to be available only in black; the Special was coloured Dove Grey, with a red and grey striped upholstered interior and several trim details changed as well. A year later, the 444's engine power output increased by a remarkable 2bhp, with another 2bhp a year later. By the end of 1950, a PV444S was priced at SKr8,100 and the twenty-five thousandth 444 left the factory in January 1952.

By 1954, the Volvo PV444H had arrived. This was the model's most significant update and featured many revisions of detail, although the basic body shape remained the same as the original 444A of 1947. The key revisions were a deepened windscreen, slimmed-down door pillars and removal of the divider between the rear window. Now, the car had a single-pane rear window of larger area, which was appreciated by many drivers, as the rear view had always been a bit restricted in the earlier versions. Only a year later, in September 1955, the PV444 was launched in the United States, and brought to production the 70bhp sports engine that had been intended for use in Volvo's first true sporting model, a car that never reached volume production.

It is time now to talk about that car, for it brought Volvo near to producing a true sporting type of car. It was during a visit in 1953 to the United States that Gabrielsson saw how popular European sports cars were, especially on the East Coast and in California. He was encouraged to visit the Californian firm of Glasspar, who had devel-oped the glass-fibre body for the then-new Chevrolet Corvette, a car destined to become America's most popular home-built sporting car ever. Glasspar was commis-sioned to produce a body design suitable for fitment to a chassis which was assembled on to Volvo PV444 running gear and using the new B14 70bhp engine. The body styling and design drawings were actually completed before Gabrielsson left the United States.

Behind the development of this first Volvo sports car was an idea in Gabrielsson's mind that he could attract the attention of those sporting car buyers in the United States to his production sedan which, incidentally, had a highly tuneable power unit. Combined with the sheer ruggedness of the PV444, it was thought that sporty-minded small sedan buyers might take a long look at the 444, which made the basis of an excellent rally car and high-performance, small road-going sedan – before blanket speed limits spoiled all that for the American motorist. The idea here, then, was to build a limited number of the P1900 and place them in high-profile locations to attract attention to Volvo.

The first prototype P1900 was built in 1953–4 and had quite an attractive line, although the front end was rather heavy, with a large radiator grille mouth that was slightly reminiscent of the Ferrari Mille Miglia and a rather oddly angular surround that did not fit in with the otherwise rounded lines of the rest of the car. In coupé form, it was, from the rear quarter, quite like the Alfa Romeo 'Villa d'Este' Coupé, but the open cars had less rounded windscreens, an improved nose, and better fitting detail. After initial evaluation, the first three cars to be built after the coupé were put on display at Torslanda Airport just outside Gothenburg. The plan, revealed at this display, was to build 300 cars for export only. After this, the prototypes were driven all round Sweden to be shown off to every Volvo dealer in the country.

After extensive testing during 1955, the P1900 went into production in January 1956. It was now equipped with a fold-down top, a more curved windscreen than the prototypes and retractable side windows. Early in March, in a promotional exercise,

Helmer Peterson and Pelle Nystrom took a P1900 to Southern Europe and North Africa on a 9.950 mile (16,000km) trip, partly to show off the car and partly to put it through a 'shake-down', to find the likely trouble spots in the car and to prove the build quality. They found more problems than they had expected, but at least those problems were found by professionals and they were able to be addressed before many more cars were built. The chassis was found to be too flexible and weak, as a result of which body mountings began to chafe through the fibreglass. Door mountings were found to be inadequate, so door closing and opening gave problems, and the general build quality was thought not to be up to Volvo standards.

After sorting out the pre-production problems, the car was on the Volvo stand at the Brussels Motor Show in January 1955 and received a reasonably warm welcome. But it was over another year before deliveries of any P1900s took place to customers and, despite Volvo relenting and allowing sales to Swedish customers, it is said that only sixty-seven cars were ever completed, thirty-eight of them being sold in the home market. That was a sad reflection of the car's potential, because it was quite an attractive-looking vehicle, though the radiator grille treatment was not to everyone's taste, but the mechanical components were well proven on the road. Perhaps it was simply that the market was not yet ready for such a car as this from a manufacturer that had a reputation for building solid and reliable cars. Even so, despite the commercial failure of the P1900, all was not lost, for the engine that was developed for it found its way into a PV444 model and a few ideas had been tested in that car along the way.

And then there was a car called 'Elizabeth', which was a very elegant creation, designed by Michelotti of Turin and built by Ghia Aigle in Switzerland. This car was built in 1953 on a PV445 chassis, especially for Gosta Wennberg, a Swedish businessman. Wennberg had met designer Michelotti at the 1952 Paris Salon and had discussed a coupé on a Volvo chassis. Michelotti had designed the car and Wennberg took the idea forward. But it all became a bit confused after that, for after the detail drawings were completed and handed over at Gothenburg, they were sent to Vignale in Turin, along with a 445 chassis. When it was realized that a mistake had been made, the chassis and drawings were transferred to Allemano in the same city, where the car was built, being delivered in June 1953. It has been suggested that there are design links between this car and the Amazon, a purely Volvo-built car.

Now, before the PV444 was discontinued, one of Volvo's most beautifully proportioned and attractive production cars ever, the Volvo 120 Amazon. But more of that later, for this chapter is concerned with the developments of the PV444 and its heir, the PV544. The 544 was announced in August 1958, after the Amazon had been on sale for almost two years, so it came as something of a surprise to the market at large. But there was a bit of a 'Beetle' syndrome to this, in that improvement of the existing model brought further sales; some of these were cult sales, while others were simply people buying the model with which they were familiar. The shape of the PV444 had certainly created a cult, especially in the United States and the 544 was taking

A PV544 early production car.

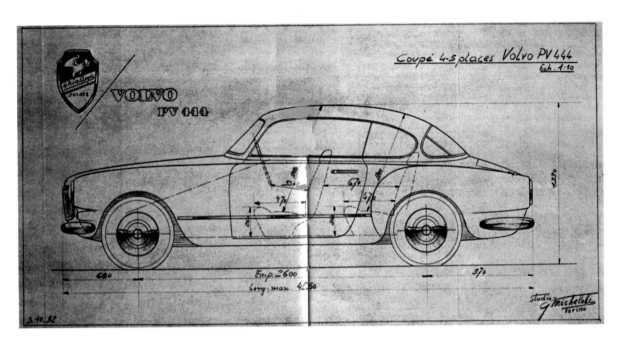

The Michelotti drawing of the PV444 coupé (known colloquially as the 'Gosta Wennberg' car, because Mr Wennberg was its sponsor).

Volvo's first serious post-war sports car, the P1900, was technologically as advanced as the Chevrolet Corvette with its glass-fibre bodywork, photographed in 1956.

*The 'Elizabeth 1' prototype, said to have been named after the
British monarch. It looks remarkably like the Boano-bodied
Alfa Romeo 1900 with an inverted radiator grille.*

*Another view of 'Elizabeth', showing how the line of this car
clearly formed the basis for the Amazon Model P121.*

*A PV544 on the East Africa Safari Rally. The first Volvo to win
this gruelling event was driven by the Singh brothers.*

advantage of that, as well as taking advantage of saving probably the SKr30,000,000 that a completely new model would have cost. With the PV544, engine performance was improved, the rear seat accommodation was improved, the windscreen was made larger and one-piece, whilst handling of this 'new car in an old shell' was vastly superior to the earlier model.

The PV544 widened the Volvo range more than ever before and also exposed it to more and more involvement in motor sport.

It was a popular saloon car racer in Europe, with leading racing driver Jo Bonnier taking to the circuits in one, as well as being a resounding success in rallying. Indeed, so successful was it in rallies, that a PV444 had taken part in the 1949 Monte Carlo Rally and a PV544 won the 1965 East African Safari Rally with the Singh brothers aboard. Tom Trana had already won the World Rally Championship in 1964, using a PV544. The PV444 and PV544 models had been the making of Volvo. Next, it was to be the turn of the Amazon.

3 The Amazon and the Development of a Sports Car

Assar Gabrielson had instructed Jan Wilsgaard to develop a concept, allocated the project number PV179, which deliberately embodied the roof line of the PV444, so as to provide a family link. Wilsgaard's resulting creation reached the road-going prototype stage, but did not appeal to everyone and so the competition was thrown open and a new car design was sought. The ultimate result was the Volvo 120 series, the 'Amazon'.

The Volvo 120 series of cars was one of the most elegant and well-proportioned car designs ever to emerge from Sweden. Styled by Jan Wilsgaard, it was the development of an assignment to produce a vehicle which combined the attributes of three earlier cars: the 'Elizabeth', Wilsgaard's own '55' design and a Helmer Petterson concept known as the the PV454. This new design had, of course, to satisfy the directors of Volvo. Working with the remit to produce a car with interior

Jan Wilsgaard's P179 almost made it to production, but the Amazon was so much better.

dimensions that would compare with such competitors as the Opel Kapitan, the Mercedes-Benz 170 series and other similarly sized European cars, Wilsgaard went to work.

Wilsgaard thought carefully about his challenge, took more than a passing look at Gosta Wennberg's Ghia-built coupe (the Elizabeth) and went back to his drawing board. The result was his design numbered "55", a car that did not carry the less-than-attractive inverted Alfa Romeo style radiator grille of the Michelotti design, but one that bore more than a passing resemblance, though was far from a direct "crib". Helmer Petterson's PV454 was, in Wilsgaard's eyes, a non-starter, as it carried too much of the PV444 in its lines and was really only a facelift of that earlier model. Wilsgaard wanted something quite new, whilst still embodying those characteristics so valued by the board of the company. He actually presented two proposals to the Volvo board and gained acceptance of the broad idea of his design, which was ultimately to be a four-door family car.

THE AMAZON ARRIVES

The design competition for the Amazon was staged out in the open by Gustaf Larson, who had seen Petterson's PV454 and, it seems, was not especially happy with what he saw. As a consequence, he instructed Wilsgaard and another stylist named Rustan Lange to produce alternatives. Lange's Type 65 was more of a four-seat coupé than family saloon car, with a large oval radiator that looked a bit like one of those oval potato slicers that was in fashion at the time. The rear end was reminiscent of a much later car built in Britain, so was certainly not cribbed, but at a glance, you could have been forgiven for thinking you were looking at a Sunbeam Rapier.

Jan Wilsgaard's Project 55, when built into a full-size model, could be seen to have quite a lot of 'Elizabeth' in it, yet there was already a hint of the 120 series in the profile. Starting out as a two-door design, the fixed aspects of his design remit were that the wheelbase of his new car was to be the same as that of the PV444 (2,600mm), it was to have four to five seats and was to have the interior attributes of its leading competitors. A preference for a split windscreen had also been expressed, though the direction that car styling was taking by 1953 did not lend itself well to this idea. Nonetheless, Wilsgaard produced two clay models, one with a full width single glass and one with a split two-piece screen. A glance at these two models left the viewer in no doubt as to which was the right choice.

Petterson's PV454, Lange's Type 65 and Wilsgaard's Type 55 were brought together for a viewing in the middle of 1953 and the outcome was an almost typical Swedish compromise. Gustaf Larson did not want to completely abandon the PV444's lines, as it had been a tremendous success story for Volvo, but yet he wanted something more modern that would sell for some years to come. So he told Jan Wilsgaard to go back to his drawing board and produce a compromise between Helmer Petterson's PV454 and his own Type 55, abandoning altogether Rustan Lange's design. Wilsgaard's reaction to that instruction was to subdue the rear fins of his original 55 design, to add a pair of doors, to borrow the concept of the split radiator grille from Petterson's 454 and to create the first model of the new Amazon.

It was immediately obvious that the tooling costs to manufacture the Amazon would make it a very expensive project to

As with all new projects, the Amazon progressed from early drawing board ideas to a clay model, after which a full-sized model would have been built.

undertake. It was not so much that the 120 would be so much more expensive a car to make, it was that the tooling costs for all aspects of the PV444 had been written off so long before, that Volvo now faced a 'culture shock' in having to invest in a complete set of press tools and components for the new model. Even so, the decision was made in early 1954 to proceed with the Amazon, with the definitive prototype being built in the summer of that year. Full-size running prototypes were built and the car was scheduled to go into production during 1956. So Wilsgaard's team was charged with creating a car for the next decade.

NEW CHAIRMAN, NEW VOLVO

As the Volvo 120 Amazon was progressing towards production status, Assar Gabrielsson was moving towards retirement. The co-founder of the company had watched the creation of what was to become Volvo's most prolific model yet and the mainstay of the company's car division for thirteen years. And out of the engineering development that went into it would be spawned the first series production sporting Volvo, but more of that a little later. The successor to Gabrielsson was a man who had spent the previous thirteen years as head of Svenska Flygmotor in Trollhattan, bringing that Volvo division to new heights of success, but a long way from the world of cars. That man was Gunnar Engellau and it was to be he who led Volvo to levels of export sales that the founders of the company could never have dreamed of.

The Amazon was a turning point for Volvo in many ways, apart from the numbers in which it was manufactured. It was to pilot an export drive to North America that began with just fifty cars in 1956 and culminated in tens of thousands of Volvos being driven along the highways of the New World. Also, this new car was to be the cornerstone of Volvo's growing reputation for building safe cars. The safety drive began in earnest with the 120 series, which had removable panels for ease of repair, front seat-belt anchorage points, as well as padding on the door cappings and

the dashboard. Seat belts were available from the car's introduction and from the very beginning, Volvo dealers promoted the sale of seat belts, so few left showrooms without them.

The engine in the Amazon was a development of the power unit from the PV444, but with an increased bore, from 75mm to 79.37mm, bringing the engine's displacement to 1,583cc from 1,414cc. With a compression ratio of 7.5:1 for the home market, the new unit produced 60bhp. One surprising element of the new car's specification was the three-speed gearbox, brought over from the 444, but to be replaced in time by a new four-speed design. The four-speed gearbox was standard from the very beginning of exports to the United States, as was the 85bhp engine, which endowed the car with a top speed of just under 92mph (148km/h) and

Two generations of Volvo – the PV544 and the new P121 Amazon together.

Jan Wilsgaard

At the age of twenty, a young Gothenburg art student was given the career break many young-sters only ever dream of. It was the result of the Volvo board's decision to establish a styling department in 1950 with the design activity at Hisingen. That young man was named Jan Wilsgaard, whose portfolio of work from the Gothenburg Art Institute so impressed Edward Lindberg, head of the design department, and Rustan Lange, chief interior designer, that he was offered the job.

Wilsgaard's first project was a large American-style sedan, to be powered by a V-8 engine and, presumably, aimed at restoring Volvo's position in the large car market, where it had been strong in Sweden before World War II. Very soon after he joined the company, this first car, code-named 'Philip', was in the metal on a jig in the factory. Presented to the Volvo board in September 1950, the 'Philip' was intended to succeed the PV60, but only one example was ever built, and that was relegated to a Volvo subsidiary in Eskilstuna as a VIP car.

A mid-sized car was Wilsgaard's next remit, this time coded P179 and aimed at replacing the PV444, retaining much of its roof line, but little else. A prototype was built, but because it was underpowered and styling had progressed some in the meantime, it too was abandoned, as its designer moved on to one of his greatest creations. He had designed a new model, labelled the 55, and out of it came the Amazon, the car which did much to confirm Volvo on the world scene. It can fairly be said that the Amazon won more new markets for Volvo than any car before it – much of that down to the design talents of Jan Wilsgaard.

Testament to Wilsgaard's expertise and ability to move with the times came with the intro-duction of the 140 series which, succeeded by the 240 line, confirmed that Volvo could still keep that long-life image it treasured, for the line remained, mildly modified in detail, for over twenty years, followed then by the immensely successful 700 series, which was launched in 1975 and then refined into the 800 series. Much of Volvo's success in the intervening years has rested on that very adventurous decision back in 1950 to appoint an inexperienced twenty-year old straight from art college.

Jan Wilsgaard, sitting at his drawing board with one of his creations.

*In Canada, this PV444 was driven from Vancouver to Halifax
by Dave Roat and Trev Jones.*

0–60mph (0–100km/h) standing start time of 16.2 seconds. Surprisingly, the 1,414cc PV444 had a better 0–60 time by almost two seconds!

In the world's export markets, the 120 proved an immediate success. The United States received it well, heralding it as a refreshing new car which was pleasant to look at, fun to drive, economical and reliable. It was, of course, a revelation after the somewhat staid looks of the PV444, though it brought with it the new 1600 engine and, though not immediately, a four-speed gearbox. These two items would carry forward the Volvo name into other products and so accelerate the company's move towards creating a truly successful sporty car, although not quite yet, as it had a new family car to settle into its markets and it was not as confident about that as it possibly should have been.

ON THE ROAD TO A SPORTS CAR

The Volvo board was clearly insecure about pinning all the company's hopes on the 120 Amazon series – not because they did not

Exports of the PV444, and then the 544, to the United States and Canada were substantial by the second half of the 1950s.

*The PV544 Sport was the ultimate version of this Viking Warrior and
was immensely popular among its users. Many still survive today.*

*This pair of P1900s shows what a pretty car it was in
roadster or hardtop form.*

think it was a good car, but because it was a quantum leap forward in style for Volvo and it was also quite a bit more expensive than the PV444. This is why, having announced that Jan Wilsgaard's beautiful creation would go into production in 1956 (although it did not actually make the dealer show-rooms until a year later), the decision was then made to 'facelift' the PV444 into the PV544, so giving the 'Forty-One Ford' style (as one American journalist described it) a new, if not extended lease of life in 1958. It was very much the American market which justified that decision as, when the engine had been uprated on the PV444 to 85bhp, the Volvo had risen to second place in the European imports league, behind Volkswagen.

The Volvo PV444 was an almost unashamed sporting machine, as it was endowed with the 70bhp, two-carburetter 1,414cc engine. Its nought-to-sixty time was said to be the best in the American market for a sub-1,500cc four-seat car, and it did not take long for the chunky little Swede to become a cult car in the fashion of the Volkswagen. *Road and Track*, in testing the engine's ability to meet the quoted 7,000rpm, took the car to a pretty astonishing 75mph (120km/h) in second gear – without valve bounce! Even remembering that the car had only a three-speed gearbox, that's a pretty stringent test. Combine that durability with the car's ability to contend with the cut and thrust (or should it be 'bash and bang', as one journalist put it?) of California traffic and it was pretty clear to see why the Volvo was endearing itself so to the North American motoring community.

By the end of the summer of 1957, the 'L' variant of the 444 had arrived in the United States with an 85bhp engine. The additional horsepower only took two-

tenths of a second off the nought-to-sixty time, but sliced a whole four seconds off nought-to-seventy (113km/h) to bring it down to 21 seconds exactly. In addition to that, top speed went up by almost 4mph (6km/h) from the 90 of the 70bhp power unit, so the sporty cult motoring fraternity was further encouraged to think that Volvo was getting sports-minded. This 85bhp Volvo continued to be sold alongside the 120 Amazon in the US for some time, vying for the affections of quite a wide range of West Coast motorists. A growing number of Americans were buying this chunky little car as a second to heavy Detroit iron, although an increasing number of enthusiastic stalwarts were actually buying it as their sole means of motorized transport.

By 1958, the sporting flavour of Volvos had become established, and so had their place in the cult car world.

The next step on the road to a real sporting Volvo was the 'facelift', the PV544, which brought to the United States the engine of the new Amazon, an 88bhp unit of 1,582cc. The higher power came at a lower top-engine speed of 5,500rpm, though the maximum speed of the car remained the same as the 'L' type PV444. Where this new unit scored was that the nought-to-sixty time dropped about a second and a half to 13 seconds exactly, whilst a further 1.2 seconds was pared off the nought-to-seventy time. The standing quarter-mile time was a pretty remarkable 19.1 seconds. Pretty remarkable, that is, when comparing this four-seat family saloon car with the much more sporting character of the Porsche 356B 1600 coupé, which turned in a nought-to-sixty time of as much as 15.3 seconds. It spoke volumes for the rather staid-looking car from Gothenburg.

Gunnar Engellau

When Assar Gabrielsson retired in 1956, his successor did not come from the automotive sector of industry, though he was a Volvo man. For thirteen years, Gunnar Engellau had been president of Svenska Flygmotor in Trollhattan. However, because he had come from the aero engine division of Volvo, it did not mean that Engellau had no appreciation for what had gone before. He was well aware that a new era had begun with his appointment , which signalled the end of the founding generation of Volvo.

In 1955, Volvo exported just fifty cars to the United States. By the end of 1956, the company had despatched 5,000 and in Engellau's first full calendar year in office, 1957, with his personal support that total rose to over 10,000. Once the export markets were opened up, there was only one way ahead for Volvo and that was expansion. This led to the building of a massive new plant on Hisingen island, adjacent to Torslanda airport. It took several years to build, but when the Torslanda plant opened in April 1964, Engellau addressed a VIP gathering which included King Gustav VI Adolf. In that address, he spoke of how much more impressive it had been for the first generation of Volvo to build 100,000 cars in twenty-three years than it could possibly be for the present generation to build 100,000 in one year. He asked that no-one should forget that it was that first generation who laid the foundations of Volvo; his generation was only building on that foundation. Sadly, Assar Gabrielsson had passed away two years before, but Gustaf Larson was there to hear that moving tribute.

Under his leadership of fifteen years, duration, Gunnar Engellau expanded Volvo's turnover ten-fold, from SKr600,000,000 in 1956 to SKr6,000,000,000 in 1971. Over that same period, 31,000 cars left Volvo factories in 1956 and 205,000 were produced in 1971. It was Engellau's leadership that brought Volvo to the attention of the world. It was he who opened up the European Economic Community to Volvo, by setting up the new truck plant at Ghent in Belgium,0 and it was under his patronage that the tremendous reputation of quality, durability and safety was enhanced.

An early complete West Bromwich built car, accompanied by Gunnar Engellau, who used an 1800 regularly as his company vehicle.

THE GERM OF A
SPORTING DESIGN

We have to go back now to 1954, briefly, to the Volvo P1900 sports car. That this model was a commercial failure did not mean that its creation had been a mistake, nor that the car was a complete disaster (though some thought it was). Indeed, there were several lessons to be drawn from its design and development. Now that Gunnar Engellau was in full control of Volvo, things were moving on apace and the Amazon was creating a stir wherever it appeared and was put on sale. Furthermore, the design experience of that 1954 period was about to bring new benefits, as Engellau decided it was time to get serious about bringing a sports car into the product range. He had seen how other manufacturers had used sporting models as 'flagships' to sell much

more mundane production types, and he decided that this same route was likely to benefit Volvo car sales.

Back in 1954, an approach had been made to the Italian coachbuilder Vignale, with a view to enlisting design work to take the pressure off the Gothenburg team. It was a developing practice to recruit the design talents and reputation of a leading styling house, as the use of the stylist's name would help to establish a charisma for a new model. At the time that Volvo approached Vignale, they were unable to help directly, but did give Gothenburg several leads and contacts for other Italian design houses. Vignale did not, as it turned out, become involved in Volvo's next sports car project either, but Engellau did go to Italy, approaching Ghia, who had been involved with Gosta Wennberg's PV444

The prototype P1800 had a very clean interior.

These are the three P958 (P1800) prototypes built by Frua in Turin.

coupé. Ghia, though, was already working in what it saw as a similar project for a competitor and so felt that it could not become involved in this Volvo project. As a result, Ghia referred Engellau to Frua, also a Turin-based concern with a significant reputation.

Before Engellau went to Frua, however, he decided to look at the design talents available to him within Volvo, and, since Helmer Petterson had been associated with the company for many years now, it seemed obvious to assign him the task of producing a series of initial design sketches. There was no certainty at that point that Volvo would appoint an Italian design house to complete the work on the new sporting car, though it seems pretty certain that Engellau had the idea of doing that from a fairly early stage. Why? Well, because apart from the fact that Volvo would not have the capacity to complete the work in-house, there was an awareness of the improved credibility with which the car would be endowed as the result of having a well-known name attached to it.

It was in 1957 that the Volvo board gave its approval for the design and construction of a new sports car prototype. It would be known initially as the P958 and its mechanical components would be sourced mainly from the Amazon parts bins, though the wheelbase would be shorter than the Amazon by 150mm, resulting in a 2,450mm dimension, though the running gear components would also be of Amazon origin. Now, Volvo's design and production were, in mid-1957, stretched to their absolute limits (vehicles were even being assembled in a disused sugar factory in Gothenburg at that time), so there would be an additional dimension to the problems of creating this new sporting model. Where, once created, would it be manufactured? The new Torslanda plant was still a long way off, the Olofstrom factory was bursting at the seams with production of the PV544 and Amazon, so somewhere else would have to be found – and that 'somewhere else' would almost certainly have to be outside Sweden. But first, the car had to be designed and approved.

THE CONCEPT IS APPROVED

Helmer Petterson had a son, Pelle, who, by 1957 was established as a boat designer, having produced an America's Cup challenger. He also had a fancy for designing a car. Petterson senior had been involved in the process of bringing the P1900 to its end, though he was still interested in seeing a sports car join the Volvo range. Now, he saw an opportunity to involve his son and so passed on to him the task of producing a series of design sketches which, by now, were to be in collaboration initially with Ghia. Those sketches were presented to the Volvo board by Petterson senior and Luigi Segre, of Ghia, as though they were the work of Helmer Petterson. The board ultimately approved the Petterson sketches, but when Gunnar Engellau discovered they were the work of Petterson junior, he was said to be furious. It seems Engellau's anger was based on the fact that he had been duped and that, much worse, Helmer Petterson had betrayed the company's confidentiality by involving his son without official approval. Whilst a compromise was reached which involved Pelle Petterson, he was certainly not given the free hand he had hoped for, as Frua was assigned the task of developing the designs and creating three prototypes. One key advantage of Frua building the prototypes was that any changes required could be made on the spot before the cars were shipped.

The final design of the car was a vehicle with quite pleasing lines. The nose end of the design presented a deep chrome-trimmed oval grille with 'egg-crate' style slatting, typical of Ferrari of the late 1950s. Two headlamps, each with a sidelight exactly below it, completed the frontal aspect. There was a large 'V' across the centre of the grille and the front bumper was split into two, each turning up about 45 degrees into the centrally positioned licence plate. In profile, the car looked longer and lower than it really was, for it had an admirable 6in (15cm) of ground clearance. The roof line was typically Italian of the time, being a long flowing line from the head of a deep sloping windscreen.

The side panels featured a smoothly rounded front wing, extending into a long front door which went down to the top of the deep side sill, while the top of the rear wing continued a horizontal line from front to rear almost to the end of the luggage compartment, then curved down into the tail end of the car. There was a chrome strip running from a position level with halfway down the headlamp along to just behind the door handle, from where it curved up to follow the top of the rear wing down to the tail lights, which were positioned horizontally. The rear bumper treatment was the same as the front, coming in from the sides and across the rear, to turn up at the licence plate in the centre. On the prototypes, the twin exhaust pipes extended through the rear valance, below the rear licence plate.

Frua completed the first prototype on time in December 1957 and invited Gunnar Engellau to visit Turin and inspect it before it was shipped to Gothenburg. He drove down from Sweden in an Amazon, with a few members of his design team to inspect the vehicle. Once the approval was given, the new car was despatched in early 1958, followed shortly afterwards by the other two. All three of the prototypes differed in minor detail, as the definitive version was being arrived at, but in general terms, the body outline was the same and was to be the established form of what was

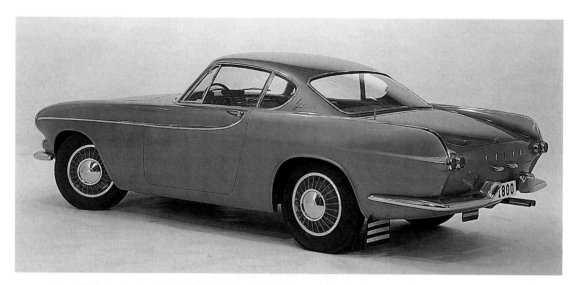

This is an early publicity photograph of an early Jensen-built car,
showing the styling of the rear flanks of the car and, despite
its Frua-style hubcaps, it has the exhaust coming out
below the rear valance.

This head-on shot shows the radiator grille of one of the prototypes.

This side view of one of the Frua prototypes was taken by Gunnar Engellau.

Pelle Petterson

Just after World War II, Volvo employed a man named Helmer Petterson as part of its design team, to work as a consultant. Petterson had worked in the United States for several years in the 1920s with the Excelsior Motor Cycle Company in Chicago, but as the Great Slump hit America, he returned to Sweden, working with GM and Ford dealers there. Spotted by Assar Gabrielsson, he walked something of a tightrope in his early career, as Gustaf Larson did not like him. However, he managed to survive the politics of that situation and went on to make a major contribution to the design of the PV444 under the direction of Erik Jern.

Petterson worked with Volvo on a number of projects, including his own design for a successor to the PV444, his PV454, which ultimately went nowhere. He also worked with Jan Wilsgaard on the P1900 sports car project, which was finally killed off by Gunnar Engellau, Gabrielsson's successor, with some support from Helmer Petterson.

Pelle Petterson was Helmer's son and had, by the 1950s, become a boat designer of some renown. For example, he had designed several competitive boats, including among them an America's Cup challenger. Now, by the mid-1950s, with the P1900 project abandoned, Pelle had shown a distinct interest in designing a sports car. But at the same time, Volvo had been in contact with Carrozzeria Ghia in Italy, with a view to asking it to produce a design for a two-plus-two sporting coupé to fulfil Volvo's needs. Ghia could not help, so subcontracted the enquiry to Frua, also in Turin. But Petterson senior had other ideas, and since he was involved in the design team, he passed the opportunity to his son, Pelle, to produce a series of sketches.

When Engellau learned that the designs he had approved had not come from Ghia, but from Helmer Petterson's son, Pelle, he was angry and almost scrapped the whole project there and then saw that the design merited retention, but had Frua build it in co-operation with Pelle Petersson. So, the young Mr Petterson's primary claim to fame in connection with Volvo was a car he nearly lost, but the car which brings his name to the fore when discussing Volvo sports cars is the 1800, a breakthrough in design for Volvo cars.

The Jensen 541 Coupé was also in build at the same time as the Volvo P1800.

to become a world-famous sporting coupé, helped a little by a British television series, but more of that later.

Now alongside the development of the new P958 coupé, the Amazon saloon was also undergoing improvements and one of those improvements was the creation of a new and larger four-cylinder engine to replace the B16B, which had first seen the light of day in the PV544. The new engine was to be labelled the B18 and was not just a revamp of the earlier power unit. It was completely new, with a bore and stroke of 84.2mm x 80mm, resulting in a displacement of 1,780cc. The water jacket allowed a greater volume of water around the cylinders for improved cooling, the big-end journals were larger than on the B16B – a feature which led the normally modest Volvo to proclaim proudly that its new engine's big ends were of larger diam-

eter than the 350bhp Ferrari V12 of the time. The compression ratio was also higher in this unit than any previous Volvo engine, at 9.5:1, which endowed it with a power output of 90bhp. Volvo's new sports car would inherit this engine and become the P1800.

THE COSMOPOLITAN SPORTS CAR

We come back now to the problems which were to be addressed by Volvo for the production of the new sporting P958. As has already been said, it was very clear that the car could not possibly be manufactured in any of the parent company's factories, so an outside subcontractor had to be found. Several avenues were explored, in mainland Europe and in Great Britain.

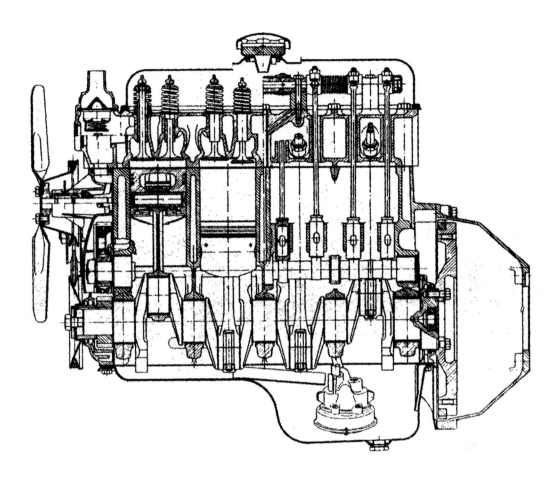

*A sectioned drawing of the early B18 engine, showing the
substantial components.*

It should be remembered that, at this time, the embryonic European Free Trade Association (EFTA) was being formed and so there was an added attraction to involving a British company in the production of the new car, because there was a reciprocal benefit to Sweden and Britain from limited tariffs and cross-trade. After an extensive search, it was decided that the major manufacturing and assembly contracts should go to two British companies.

The Pressed Steel Company, a British Motor Corporation division, would have the task of producing the major pressings and assemblies of the P1800, whilst actual build and finish would be contracted to Jensen Motors Limited, a small family-run car maker located in West Bromwich, just to the north-west of Birmingham in the heart of Britain's industrial West Midlands. Jensen was a limited production car manufacturer, its current model of the time being the 541, a large grand

The Jen-Tug was a small tractive unit sold by Jensen in some numbers to parcel carriers and operators of small articulated freight vehicles, such as car transporters. Here's one carrying Austin A40 Sports models from the factory (seen across the road in the background) to a storage area.

touring car powered by a Chrysler engine. Jensen also had the contract to assemble the Austin Healey 3000 model sports car for the British Motor Corporation, so had an established reputation in that field. As a result, Volvo designers and production technicians were despatched from Gothenburg to West Bromwich to set up an assembly, quality control and despatch programme for the Volvo P1800.

Volume manufacture of the P1800 was planned to begin in earnest in the spring of 1961. It would prove to be one of the most cosmopolitan vehicles of its time and could claim to be the precursor of the true world car in terms of manufacturing. Today, many cars are produced in just this fashion, but Volvo can be said to have been the

true pioneer of this concept. Design came from Sweden and Italy; the power plant would be made in Sweden, with components from Great Britain and Germany; the transmission would come from Sweden, with parts from Great Britain and the United States; pressings and panels would be made in Britain and final assembly would also be in that country, whilst Italian tyres made in Britain completed the production.

Whilst Pressed Steel Fisher was to manufacture the body pressings and Jensen was to assemble the cars, other British manufacturers included Vandervell, who supplied the big-end shell bearings for the engine, whilst SU carburetters were fitted. Girling manufactured the brake components, Sankey of Wellington made the road wheels and Laycock de Normanville provided the electrically actuated overdrive for the Swedish-made gearbox. The British Pirelli company supplied the Cinturato tyres from its Burton-on-Trent factory. The lighting and general electrical installation came from Joseph Lucas, though the ignition parts came from Bosch in Germany. The steering gear, alternator and starter motor also came from Germany, whilst the Delco shock absorbers and Spicer rear axle were sourced in the United States.

Jensen's initial contract was for the production of 10,000 cars, with final inspection and quality control being entirely under the eye of Volvo personnel. For quite some time, cars were to be shipped from West Bromwich to Gothenburg for examination, with detail rectification work undertaken where necessary, before being despatched to their market destinations. This even happened to cars destined for sale in Great Britain. So, at last, Volvo's new sporting car was born and, co-incidentally, the value of EFTA was being put to proof.

4 From Prototypes to Production

It was never anticipated that the prototype Volvo P985s (P1800s by the time the world was made aware of their existence) built by Frua would be the definitive production design, for even the three prototypes differed in detail from each other. What was more, they were to undergo further changes at Gothenburg before production at West Bromwich would begin. Even at that, the first car built by Jensen Motors in 1960 was shipped to Gothenburg for close examination and detail revisions before the final go-ahead was given and full production began.

PRE-PRODUCTION CHANGES

The P1800 which appeared at the Brussels Salon, in April 1960, was the second prototype and had most of the detail features that were common to all three prototypes. However, many of these details were abandoned or underwent change for the production models which would leave Jensen's West Bromwich factory. For example, the large stylized 'V' that appeared on the radiator grilles of all three prototypes was considered an unnecessary detail and so was abandoned for production models. The artificial spoked-wheel-effect hubcaps were also dropped, partly for cost and partly for appearance reasons.

Other detail changes were made for production, costing or service reasons, rather than any revision in cosmetic effect. A typical service consideration was the positioning of the exhaust tailpipes. It was decided that having them exit through the rear valance was not a good idea from a number of points of view, the principal one being that damage to the valance could result from having two bits of metal sticking through it. For example, if the tailpipes were to come loose for any reason, then they would move about and inevitably strike the panel, so causing unnnecessary damage. Something striking the underside of the car could move the whole exhaust system, or a minor 'shunt' could push the tailpipes out of their normal position, so causing damage to the valance. And from a production timing point of view, it simply would take more time to ensure accurate positioning, which would add to production time, and so add to cost. As a result, the exhaust system was modified.

Other purely production cost improvements were made to the P1800, too. It was decided that an opening rear quarter light was a luxury the owner could live without in the interests of keeping the price down, so that item was dropped. The instrument panel was examined again and it was decided that a slightly less futuristic set of dials and switches would most probably be preferred by customers in a wide range of markets. What was more, such a change would result in further cost savings. A similar approach was

Rear end of one of the prototypes showing the exhaust with two pipes through the rear valance.

taken to the rear bumpers. In this case, since the exhaust pipes would no longer protrude through the rear valance, between the inner ends of the rear half bumpers, there was no longer a need (if ever there had been) to turn the inner ends up in the way they were, quite apart from the fact that there was now a vacant gap where the exhaust pipes had been, so it was thought that the use of a horizontal bumper would be easier to fit on the production line and so would cost less. Trim and seat changes, on the other hand, were simply a part of the process of evolution from prototype to production model.

In the process of creating an equitable selling price for the P1800, it was decided that there should be two gearbox options. A fourth-speed overdrive had been visualized from the days when Frua developed Pelle Petterson's sketches into a real car. This allowed the four-speed Amazon gearbox to be adapted for use in the new sporting model, endowing it with an extra speed for top-end performance, without the added cost of a new gearbox design – besides which, five-speed gearboxes were not yet in common use, even in sports cars. From a

The rear end of a production model, showing its exhaust below the rear valance, yet retaining the prototype-style bumper.

production standpoint, however, the cost of an overdrive unit would increase the basic selling price of the car. The solution was to offer the basic four-speed gearbox as a standard part of the specification, with the overdrive as an optional extra. This would keep the basic price down, especially for the US market, where price competition from British sports cars, such as the MGA 1600 coupé, was already very stiff.

JENSEN GOES TO WORK

Jensen Motors Limited was established by two brothers, Alan and Richard Jensen, in 1934, as a process of buying out an old bodybuilding firm, W J Smith and Sons in Carters Green, West Bromwich. Their early production was truck bodies, progressing to light passenger-carrying coachwork and vans then, thinking there was more business for them in car bodies, they progressed to producing custom bodies for Morris, Singer, Standard and Wolseley chassis. They built a convertible on a Ford V-8 chassis for film star Clark Gable in 1935, the first true Jensen in the eyes of enthusiasts. Next came the 'S' Type Jensen in 1936 and more models up to World War II. Armoured cars were their contribution to the war effort, then a return to the world of cars after the conflict.

In the 1950s, the Austin Motor Company subcontracted Jensen to assemble the Austin A40 convertible, their first venture into volume subcontracting and a design based on the 1950 Jensen Interceptor. In 1952, Leonard Lord, Austin's chief executive, awarded Jensen the contract for assembly of the Austin-Healey 100/4 sports car. The Austin-Healey contract continued throughout the life of the 100 series and the 3000 models. In the meantime, they developed their own Chrysler V-8-engined sporting coupé, the 541, and by 1957, had moved from Carters Green to a new factory in Kelvin Way. Clearly they had the skills and experience that AB Volvo was looking for in the assembly of their new sporting coupé, the P1800. So the contract was won.

Once the feature details of the P1800 were resolved, the task of putting the car into volume production was heavily dependent upon Jensen being able to establish and assure the supply chain with Pressed Steel Fisher and the component suppliers with whom it would be in contact for the assembly of the Swedish car. Most of the components were coming from sources not far from West Bromwich, but the body units and pressings had to travel a long way, from Linwood in Scotland, and so the supply line between the two factories had to be reliable. The British motor industry was enduring labour relations problems, though one of the blackest patches was currently behind them, so it seemed it was not going to be a bed of roses for the small West Bromwich firm from the beginning. The Swedes were not fully aware of the extent of the tensions between shop floor and management and, perhaps a little naively, expected a contract to be met according to the agreed conditions, without interruption and without shortfalls in performance or standards.

The first Jensen-built car emerged on time and was despatched by means of a British Air Ferries Bristol Freighter to Sweden for assessment and approval, as well as final verification of the production specification. That it was approved is now a matter of record, though clearly everyone at Pressed Steel and Jensen worked especially hard to make sure there were no hitches or quality problems. The target production rate was fifty cars a week, which was a higher rate than Jensen had ever produced before from their small West Bromwich factory. It was, in fact, the biggest undertaking of the company's history and Jensen was about to face problems of a magnitude it could not have anticipated.

Of major consequence to Jensen's board was how they would finance the expansion of their manufacturing floorspace without forfeiting any of the work they were already engaged in, for they were still producing their own cars as well as the

The Jensen factory on Kelvin Way, in West Bromwich, was a significant advance on the old Smith coachworks and was a modern, well-equipped factory.

Austin-Healey 3000, and planned to continue doing so. As a result, they would have to more than double their manufacturing capacity to take on the Volvo project. It would appear that the banks were not sufficiently interested in giving the extent of support needed, so outside captial was sought, which effectively meant selling the assets of the company to outsiders, a step reluctantly taken in order to get on with the job.

Another aspect which would have a telling effect on the fortunes of this contract was the fact that the production contract for the body-shells and pressings was made directly between Volvo and Pressed Steel. It was linked to, but separate from, the agreement with Jensen, so Jensen's extent of control over what Pressed Steel did was only ever in a monitoring capacity as an agent. Any major problems which arose were really the province of Volvo to resolve, but no management team likes to be thought of as unable to control a situation placed in its care, so often Jensen was blamed for Pressed Steel's shortfalls. This was to develop into quite a serious problem for the West Bromwich company and it was

one they would never completely resolve.

Other subcontractors in Britain included Laycock, Lucas, SU and Vandervell, none of which, despite all being larger companies than Jensen, gave many problems, either in supply chain or quality terms. The American and German suppliers worked on theoretically longer lead times, so running stocks were kept at higher levels, which meant that any short-term delays in deliveries were cushioned by West Bromwich stockholdings. It was the relationship with Pressed Steel which gave the real cause for concern. It would begin with minor inconsistencies in deliveries and detail shortfalls in finish quality which Jensen, as prime contractor, would have to resolve to Volvo's satisfaction. That the pressings contract was not between Jensen and Pressed Steel did not help, because Volvo had to become involved from time to time and this put Jensen under the spotlight, leaving its management team vulnerable to accusations of being unable to manage the contract. The result was that on many occasions, Jensen would 'cover up' and if a quality problem arose, attempt to deal with it rather than throw it back.

Behind closed doors! A prototype P1800 photographed at the Jensen factory at West Bromwich.

LET PRODUCTION COMMENCE

The original system set up for production at West Bromwich was that Pressed Steel would supply 'dressed' (semi-finished) bodyshells and sundry panels to Jensen on skids and in quantities that would at least match Jensen's required output of fifty cars per week. Jensen would then clean, degrease and apply all paint, from primer undercoat to finish coat, all in cellulose. The amount of pre-paint preparation was intended to be minimal for Jensen, and so it was at the beginning of the production run. After painting, Jensen would then

assemble the cars, with engine/transmission units coming in from Sweden and all the other components from their various sources.

It must have been a logistics nightmare for a firm that had never had to deal with such a widespread supply chain, even though most of the components for its own range of grand touring cars were sourced from outside, including the engine and transmission from the United States. However, this was one of the factors which had impressed Volvo during their negotiations with Jensen. Jensen had shown itself to be capable of dealing with the giants of Detroit, as well as the major British component suppliers. It had also proved its ability to assemble under subcontract with the Austin-Healey 100 and 3000. Despite demanding production schedules, Jenson had maintained a high standard of quality, such as must have impressed Volvo.

As production advanced, so problems began to arise. Firstly, it was with surface finish, where Jensen was often blamed for failing to ensure that metal surfaces were adequately prepared. These early problems were passed over, though it must have caused a few difficulties for Gothenburg, as rectification had to take place in Sweden, in view of the fact that all cars were at that time being returned to Gothenburg before their despatch to various world markets. This was not what Volvo had expected. Certainly, minor rectifications and damage repair were part of the plan, but not production remedial work. But Jensen was not able to enforce better quality standards on Pressed Steel, because it did not have available either the opportunity, or even

the threat, to go elsewhere and its supplier knew it. So too little was done and Jensen was left to 'carry the can'.

In Great Britain, the press was euphoric about the fact that this new Volvo was to be manufactured in Linwood and in West Bromwich. Most journalists of the day took the view that Jensen Motors had more than adequate experience of assembling this type of car, although not in such numbers as Volvo was seeking, by way of having built the Austin A40 sports (a scaling down of Volvo's own Interceptor design in 1952), the big Austin-Healey sports car, as well as having been involved in work on the Austin A90 Atlantic and building cars of its own design. No critical comments were raised by the press of the day to suggest that Jensen was anything less than entirely competent for the task it was about to undertake. And so it progressed.

It had always been Volvo's plan to have the first 250 cars shipped to Gothenburg

The first 1800 built at West Bromwich was air-freighted to Gothenburg via British Air Ferries for inspection before series production began.

for inspection and verification. Thereafter, the intention was that Jensen should ship cars to their worldwide destinations directly from West Bromwich, so keeping down the final cost of the product. However, after several early panel fit and part/panel finish problems, there was a major discussion at Kelvin Way about how Jensen was not upholding agreed quality standards. Clearly, the Jensen board defended their company's actions vigorously, for it was obvious that assembly workers at West Bromwich could only assemble what they were given. Certainly, anything but perfect fit and finish could, and perhaps should, have been thrown back at Pressed Steel, though production numbers were a high priority and so compromises were made. It would appear that Pressed Steel was not especially helpful to Jensen here, preferring to avoid any confrontation with its own work force, with which it was treading a very delicate path at that time anyway.

Out of the quality conference which ensued, and after a board meeting at Gothenburg, came the resolution that Volvo would station a permanent quality control assessor at West Bromwich. Jensen was not averse to this proposition, feeling that the permanent pressure of a Volvo man at Kelvin Way would go some way towards vindicating its position. Volvo had already recognized that the Pressed Steel output was not up to standard, but without incurring a huge cost, it was not possible to withdraw production from Linwood and transfer it elsewhere, especially since Jensen had no pressing facilities. Pressed Steel was clearly aware of the strength of its position, and it has been claimed that it did too little about its own product quality, probably in the knowledge that, firstly, it had too little control over its production workforce to enforce improvements, and, secondly, it may well have been thought that the company had Volvo over a

barrel. Whatever the thinking at Linwood, the consequences of its product quality failures fell firmly on to Jensen Motors.

PAPERING OVER THE CRACKS

Few of the problems to beset Jensen in those early days reached the press, for it was not in either Jensen's or Volvo's interests to tell the world that they were having quality problems. So, in July 1961, when the British public was seeing more and more about this new Swedish sports car, there came a report from *The Autocar* magazine in Great Britain. Praising the fact that more than 50 per cent of the Swedish car was being made in Great Britain, the reporter went on to tell his readers how Jensen had expanded its factory in Kelvin Way at West Bromwich to accommodate production of the new Volvo P1800 at a rate of up to 150 cars per day.

To put it mildly, the suggestion that Jensen could even begin to produce as many as 150 cars a day was a preposterous exaggeration, for such a production level would have meant that Jensen would build 37,500 cars a year, which is almost as many coupés as were produced in the whole life of the car. As it was, only 400 cars had been built by the time this article was published, which actually only respesented four months' production. Allowing that the article may have been written up to a month before it appeared, say June, it was clear that the production rate was already several months behind schedule. This in itself was not a new experience, for Volvo or any other car maker, but in this case it was a sign, for those who knew, that all was not as it should be.

It was also being reported that 'a staff of Swedish inspectors' was being based at

Kelvin Way to ensure that: 'the job is done in accordance with Volvo precepts'. Again, this was quite a way from the actual facts of the situation, though clearly the reporter had visited the West Bromwich factory in the period in which these early problems were being addressed and when Volvo personnel were at West Bromwich in some numbers. Nevertheless, both Volvo and Jensen personnel were able to remain tight-lipped enough to prevent any hint of the troubles escaping to the press. Quite clearly, both companies still wanted this arrangement to work and recognized that any adverse leaks of information could have a detrimental effect on sales.

EARLY PRESS FEEDBACK

An American magazine called *Motor Life* despatched journalist Douglas Armstrong from his base in England to West Bromwich to follow a P1800's journey from Jensen's factory to Gothenburg. After being inspected and passed off, he would take the car out on a road test. Clearly, Mr Armstrong was impressed, for after driving the car on auto routes, secondary roads and Sweden's unmade gravel surfaced country roads, he reported that this was a quality sports car that handled well. He found a remarkably low noise level in the car on auto routes and a surefootedness on unmade roads that was creditable of much

A front quarter view of a Jensen-built P1800 in Sweden.

more expensive machinery. He reported that, even on the unmetalled roads, with their unnervingly deep ditches on either side, that the Pirellis held the car just where the driver wanted it to be. It was, in the opinion of Mr Armstrong, a car that would give faultless performance and reliability five years hence.

There was not the slightest hint in Douglas Armstrong's report that this P1800 was in any way the product of an already troubled working relationship between Jensen and Volvo. Indeed, he commented most favourably on the finish of the car and thought that, for a price of $3,800, there would be a ready market for this multinational Volvo. Proof of that statement came as, in the words of *Car and Driver* magazine: 'hundreds of long-suffering enthusiasts who wrote cheques for $3,800' began to receive their much prized vehicles.

Car and Driver has always been inclined towards the cynical, pulling no punches in its assessment of new cars com-

ing into the US market. In September 1961, its report on the Volvo P1800 was no exception. It referred to the 'reintroduction' of the car, which is correct if you consider that it was first exposed to the American public at the New York Auto Show in April 1960 and was only becoming available to the market place in September 1961. But, just as Volvo had done many years before with the much-delayed PV444, those buyers who had ordered the car at $3,800 received their cars at the price they had been asked to pay upon its announcement. *Car and Driver* went on to observe that the P1800 had been labelled 'star of the show' at New York in 1960, noting that even when the car was 're-introduced' a year later, interest was unabated, though clearly the element of surprise had been somewhat dulled.

This *Car and Driver* road research report continued in a more charitable context now, offering the view that the new Volvo was a breakthrough because, until its announcement, attractive two/four-seat

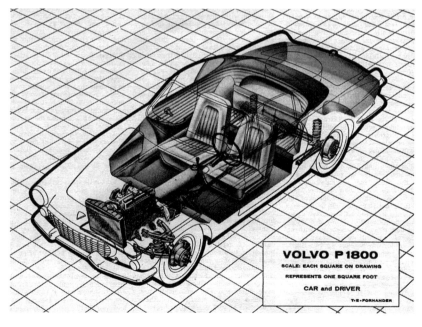

LEFT: Car and Driver *magazine's cutaway drawing of a P1800, showing where everything is located in the car.*

RIGHT: An end section view of the P1800 engine.

coupés capable of over 100mph cost $4,000 and up (usually, as the writer put it: 'very up!'). The biggest obstacle to sales of the P1800 in the United States was, according to this report, the low availability of cars for delivery. Out on the road, the new car was found to be generally smooth, though the test vehicle had its engine idle speed set a little low which made it a rather lumpy when stuck in stationary traffic on the hottest day of the year in New York's streets. Despite that, the engine was thought to be 'unbreakable' up to the 6,000rpm red line. *Car and Driver* came out thoroughly convinced that here was a car of excellent value, high performance and very solid construction. In particular, the finish of the car was highly praised, so

clearly Jensen was, for the most part, 'getting it right' by the summer of 1961.

Now *Road and Track* was actually the first of America's motor sporting journals to road test the P1800, in March 1961, observing that the new car's principal adversaries would be the Porsche 356 and the Alfa Romeo Giulietta Sprint. It was described as a 'civilized touring car for people who want to travel rapidly in style'. The report went on to liken travel in the Volvo to that of the Ferrari or Aston Martin, but at much more modest cost. Commenting on the bodywork, the area of most interest to Jensen Motors, *Road and Track* complimented both design and finish, again making no comment on any product quality problems.

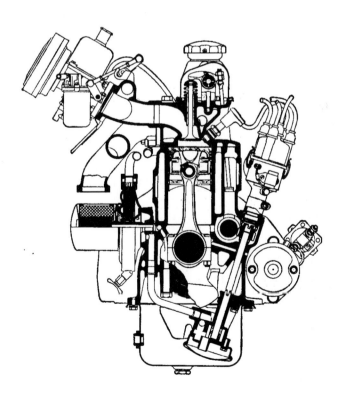

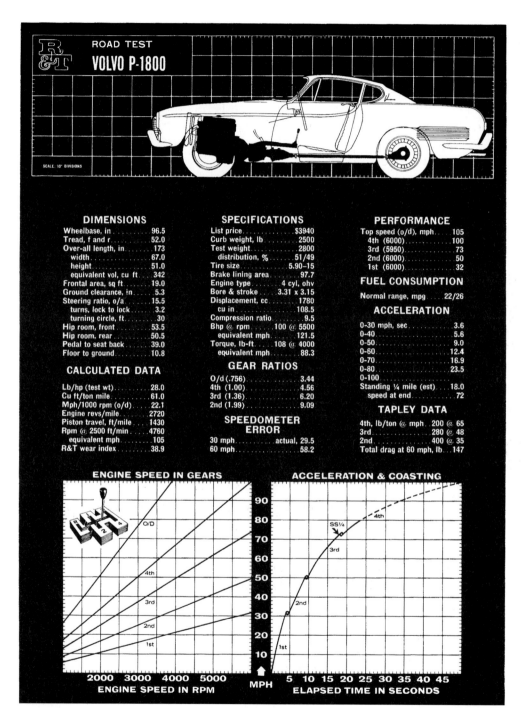

ROAD TEST
VOLVO P-1800

SCALE: 10" DIVISIONS

DIMENSIONS

Wheelbase, in	96.5
Tread, f and r	52.0
Over-all length, in	173
width	67.0
height	51.0
equivalent vol, cu ft	342
Frontal area, sq ft	19.0
Ground clearance, in	5.3
Steering ratio, o/a	15.5
turns, lock to lock	3.2
turning circle, ft	30
Hip room, front	53.5
Hip room, rear	50.5
Pedal to seat back	39.0
Floor to ground	10.8

CALCULATED DATA

Lb/hp (test wt)	28.0
Cu ft/ton mile	61.0
Mph/1000 rpm (o/d)	22.1
Engine revs/mile	2720
Piston travel, ft/mile	1430
Rpm @ 2500 ft/min	4760
equivalent mph	105
R&T wear index	38.9

SPECIFICATIONS

List price	$3940
Curb weight, lb	2500
Test weight	2800
distribution, %	51/49
Tire size	5.90–15
Brake lining area	97.7
Engine type	4 cyl, ohv
Bore & stroke	3.31 x 3.15
Displacement, cc	1780
cu in	108.5
Compression ratio	9.5
Bhp @ rpm	100 @ 5500
equivalent mph	121.5
Torque, lb-ft	108 @ 4000
equivalent mph	88.3

GEAR RATIOS

O/d (.756)	3.44
4th (1.00)	4.56
3rd (1.36)	6.20
2nd (1.99)	9.09

SPEEDOMETER ERROR

30 mph	actual, 29.5
60 mph	58.2

PERFORMANCE

Top speed (o/d), mph	105
4th (6000)	100
3rd (5950)	73
2nd (6000)	50
1st (6000)	32

FUEL CONSUMPTION

Normal range, mpg	22/26

ACCELERATION

0-30 mph, sec	3.6
0-40	5.6
0-50	9.0
0-60	12.4
0-70	16.9
0-80	23.5
0-100	
Standing ¼ mile (est)	18.0
speed at end	72

TAPLEY DATA

4th, lb/ton @ mph	200 @ 65
3rd	280 @ 48
2nd	400 @ 35
Total drag at 60 mph, lb	147

ENGINE SPEED IN GEARS

O/D
4th
3rd
2nd
1st

ENGINE SPEED IN RPM
2000 3000 4000 5000

ACCELERATION & COASTING

4th
SS¼
3rd
2nd
1st

MPH

ELAPSED TIME IN SECONDS
5 10 15 20 25 30 35 40 45

Road & Track's *road-test findings for the early P1800.*

Autocar road test • No. 1884

Make · VOLVO   Type · P1800

Manufacturer : AB Volvo, Göteborg, Sweden
Concessionaires : Volvo Concessionaires, Ltd., 28 Albemarle Street, London, W.1.

Test Conditions
Weather ... Dry and sunny with 7-20 m.p.h. wind
Temperature .... 56 deg. F. (13 deg. C.)
Barometer .... 29·9in. Hg.
Dry tarmac and concrete surfaces.

Weight
Kerb weight (with oil, water and half-full fuel tank)
22 cwt (2,464lb-1,118 kg)
Front-rear distribution, per cent F, 54·2; R, 45·8
Laden as tested ...... 25 cwt (2,800lb-1,270kg)

Turning Circles
Between kerbs .... L, 32ft 4in.; R, 33ft. 5in.
Between walls ...... L, 34ft 5in.; R, 35ft. 6in.
Turns of steering wheel lock to lock .... 3·25

Performance Data
Overdrive top gear m.p.h. per 1,000 r.p.m. ... 21·0
Top gear m.p.h. per 1,000 r.p.m. .... 15·0
Mean piston speed at max. power ... 2,887 ft/min.
Engine revs. at mean max. speed ...... 4,880 r.p.m.
B.h.p. per ton laden 72

FUEL AND OIL CONSUMPTION

FUEL................................Premium Grade
(97 octane RM)
Test Distance........................1,245 miles
Overall Consumption .... 24·9 m.p.g.
(11·35 litres/100 km)
Normal Range .... 24–32 m.p.g.
(11·77-8·83 litres/100 km)
OIL: SAE 30 ... Consumption: 10,000 m.p.g.

MAXIMUM SPEEDS AND ACCELERATION (mean) TIMES

1/4 MILE — 19·1 sec

MAXIMUM SPEEDS		
GEAR	m.p.h.	k.p.h.
O.D. TOP (mean)	102·5	164·9
(best)	104	166·4
TOP	90	144·8
3rd:	67	108
2nd:	45	72
1st:	28	45

TIME IN SECONDS: 4·4 6·7 9·6 13·2 18·3 24·6 35·2
TRUE SPEED m.p.h.: 0 30 40 50 60 70 80 90 100
CAR SPEEDOMETER: 30 41 51 62 73 83·5 95 105

Speed range and time in seconds

m.p.h.	O.D. Top	Top	3rd	2nd	1st
10—30	—	8·6	6·2	4·5	—
20—40	—	8·4	5·8	4·1	—
30—50	—	8·3	6·1	—	—
40—60	—	8·3	6·7	—	—
50—70	14·8	9·3	—	—	—
60—80	15·2	11·4	—	—	—
70—90	19·6	16·2	—	—	—

BRAKES
(from 30 m.p.h. in neutral)

Pedal load	Retardation	Equiv. distance
25lb	0·35g	86ft
50lb	0·65g	47ft
75lb	0·90g	33·6ft
Hand brake	0·33g	92ft

CLUTCH   Pedal load and travel 45lb and 5·5in.

HILL CLIMBING AT STEADY SPEEDS

2nd: 1 in 4·2
3rd: 1 in 6·3
Top: 1 in 8·9
O.D. Top: 1 in 11·7

GEAR	O.D.			
PULL (lb per ton)	Top 190	Top 250	3rd 350	2nd 520
Speed Range (m.p.h.)	54–60	48–53	35–45	28–35

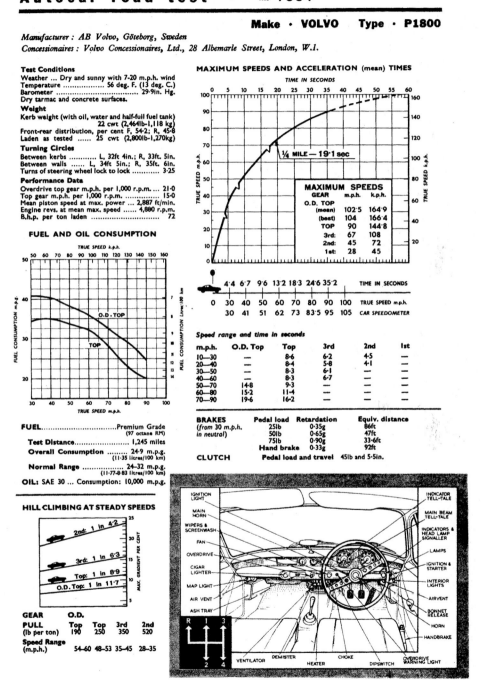

The Autocar *road-test report on the P1800.*

After a technical review of the P1800 in March 1961, which thoroughly praised the project, its design and concept, a second road test was conducted just a year later. That second road test was not of a prototype, but of a car taken from the flow of vehicles coming into the United States to satisfy those long-standing orders, many going back to the 1960 New York Auto Show. That 1962 road test explained how a combination of events, including a string of labour disputes throughout the industry, conspired to delay commencement of production and deliveries. But, finally, the car was out and finding new friends among its customers. Again, there was no comment on panel or paint finish standards, so quite clearly the problem was being kept under control and the Volvo P1800 was making its mark.

5 Teething Troubles – Production in Sweden

In the earliest days of P1800 production in Great Britain, Volvo was willing to concede that teething troubles would account for a certain level of quality problems in production, especially since the pressings were being produced and raw-assembled in one place, whilev the car was being assembled and finished four hundred-odd miles away. Inevitably, it is always difficult to pinpoint exact responsibility for a given defect after a car has been finished. However, it is clear that there were serious problems in the production sequence of the P1800 which caused Volvo to decide that its best route was the production of the car in Sweden under its own direct control.

IN TROUBLED WATERS

In hindsight, it seems clear that Jensen Motors took on a contract that was far too big for the company to manage easily. That the Jensen brothers had to sell a major part of their shareholding in their company so as to raise capital for the Volvo venture is sign enough that they were financially weaker than necessary for such a major undertaking. On the other hand, they had all the right experience to impress Volvo into believing that they could do the job. In fact, the Jensen company was certainly technically competent to take on the contract, as it had proved with its work for the

Here is a P1800 body assembled from the Pressed Steel body set, but clearly showing several faults in the original pressings.

73

British Motor Corporation in building the Austin-Healey sports cars and in creating the Austin A40 sports model out of its own Interceptor design.

It might be said that Jensen's management was not up to the job, being too weak to control the contract with Pressed Steel Company Limited. Yet the small West Bromwich firm had managed to buy engines and transmissions from one of the American giants, Chrysler, with considerable success and controlled the supply contracts very well. However, that was rather different, in that Jensen was buying an existing product, virtually 'off the shelf' and in significantly smaller numbers than the components required from Linwood. In addition, the customers for the Jensen 541 were essentially 'personal' customers who would accept more readily any delays in delivery of individual cars, whereas the Volvo contract was with a large corporate entity that was concerned with achieving production numbers.

It is true to say that Jensen found the control of the Pressed Steel contract very difficult, for here it was not buying something 'off the shelf', but finishing a product for another, much larger, corporation. In corporate size, Pressed Steel, too, was much larger than Jensen and had been plagued with labour difficulties that were not familiar to Jensen. It would be unfair to say that, as a result, project management was not Jensen's forte, but they clearly had no experience of project management on such a scale and it inevitably cost them dearly. Indeed, one of the reasons this project was ultimately lost was Jensen's inability to enforce adherence to quality and delivery targets.

The Pressed Steel Company had problems, too, for it was having to wrestle with serious industrial relations battles at a time when it was also trying to interpret and apply Volvo's press tool drawings for the production of the 'raw' body units. Naturally enough, Volvo's drawings were dimensioned in millimetres, whilst the British motor industry used imperial measurements, so the company either had to 'metricate' the design and the production teams, or allow them to continue converting dimensions (or guess) as they worked. Often the latter course was followed in the interests of expedience, not least because there was no time, or particular incentive, to train men up to metrication so long before there was a political motive in Great Britain to do so. Therefore, most of the Pressed Steel teams were still orientated towards feet and inches for dimensions and non-metric threads.

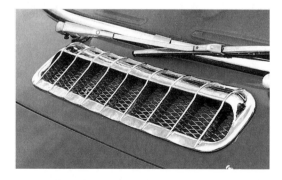

The early scuttle air vent of the P1800 – chrome-plated.

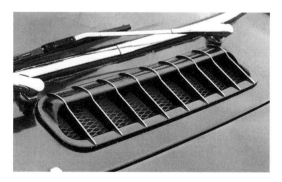

Later, scuttle vents were painted, to deter reflections into the car.

The 1800S brought a different air vent, devoid of the scoops.

The Pressed Steel contract was placed in the expectation that it would quickly arrive at a production agreement with the workforce that would uphold the quality standards and volume expected by Volvo. Sadly, that did not work out as the company found itself, along with much of the rest of the British motor industry, embroiled in a series of disputes which virtually brought car production to a standstill. The result was that a production flow which should have started in the middle of 1960 began as a trickle almost a year later. We have already covered those awesome start-up problems from Jensen's point of view and have touched on the Pressed Steel side of the story, too. There was a running argument throughout the contract about who was responsible for what in the areas of metal preparation and finishing. Panel clearances, too, were a frequent topic of conversation, dependent upon who was inspecting batches released to Jensen at any given time.

It is sad to reflect that there were periodic misinterpretations of dimensions on the line and examples of poorly finished body units leaving Linwood, but much of this was not helped by the fact that the workers at Jensen, feeling it was not their job, often found themselves dressing welds and perhaps, on occasions, not taking as much care as they might have done, often under the pressure of time. The result? A

rectification in Gothenburg, the realization of the practical problems of using incompatible finish paint materials (Jensen worked in cellulose, whilst Volvo used synthetic paints), and a cost which had to be put at somebody's door!

Another aspect of the problem was that there had never been at Linwood the kind of team spirit that had existed for many years at West Bromwich. However, as a consequence of expanding its workforce so quickly, Jensen was also losing some of that comradeship. Whilst the West Bromwich firm had enjoyed a fine reputation for the quality of its own cars and in the business of subcontracted car assembly, the speed with which the company had expanded to fulfil the Volvo contract must have placed severe limitations on its ability to maintain that working spirit and, as new workers began to outnumber the older team, so pride in Jensen Motors became ever more difficult to uphold.

THE CARS THAT JENSEN BUILT

Despite the problems encountered by Jensen in the process of building the cars it produced for Volvo, an average of 2,000 per year were built at West Bromwich – something significantly short of the target, but

The Frua-designed hub-cap on the prototypes.

This was the hub-cap fitted to West Bromwich-built cars.

sufficient cars to impress journalists and public alike. The quality problems were generally overcome before any cars reached the public and the press was either generous to Jensen or they also saw only cars that were up to scratch.

Once Volvo's own quality controller was established at Kelvin Way, the likelihood of below-standard cars was, in any event, diminished. He also was going to witness for himself the kinds of rectifications that fell to theJensen workers to carry out before they could do any of their own work.

Cars out of the gate were the primary barometer of Jensen's success and the company's handling of the extensive post-prototype modification programme was a major part of achieving that goal. That first stage was completed with the absolute minimum of problems and Volvo was pleased with Jensen's performance in that area. Now, the target was to get those cars out of the gate and to absorb the task of production modifications on the way. As has already been explained earlier, the problems which beset the start of quantity manufacture were not of Jensen's making or within its control. In the United States, where the largest single crop of orders had been taken, customer satisfaction was high as the cars began to trickle through, a situation no doubt aided by Volvo's commitment to meet those orders at the price originally set of $3,800. It lost money, but it strengthened customer loyalty and enhanced Volvo's reputation in a market already very important to them.

Coming back to the prototypes briefly, it will be remembered that several relatively minor changes were made to the car in order to prepare it for production. As the engineering drawings were advanced to production stage, a few more modifications were made. For example, the fuel tank filler cap was relocated from the right side to the left side of the car – convenient for owners of right-hand drive examples, as it placed the filler on the kerb side of the road, but an odd decision for the vast majority of left-hand drive examples, as it put it on the driver's side. That would be no problem on the modern filling station fore-court, but many countries still had little local garages which had their fuel pumps on the roadside. This was the case, even in the United States, so it meant you could have to stretch the filler hose over the car bodywork and perhaps risk damage to paintwork.

Other modifications introduced as the production process moved closer were aimed at cost-cutting, consistent always with maintaining safety standards. One area where safety was carefully considered before making the economy was the brakes. The prototypes had been designed with rear brake shoes of 223sq cm of sur-face contact area. After careful considera-tion of the possible consequences, it was decided that a narrower shoe could be safe-ly fitted, reducing the braking surface con-tact area to 210sq cm while having an insignificant effect on the performance of the brakes on the road. It saved a few more kronor.

After the brakes came the air vent on the top of the scuttle, just ahead of the windscreen. Because it was felt necessary to modify the vent itself, so as to improve its ability to draw air, the opportunity was taken to employ a less elaborate grille, again with a resultant cost saving. Inside, the question was asked whether the owner could live without door pockets, as the manufacture of the door trim panels was going to cost less without the pockets than with them. This was simply because there was a small reduction in material cost, but a worthwhile reduction in time for produc-tion, so the door pocket went the way of a

When P1800 production transferred to Sweden, the hub-caps took on a different style again.

number of other features of the prototypes. In place of the door pockets, a pair of moulded bins were fitted alongside the footwells. The hubcaps became less elabo-rate than those of the prototypes as well, so the production costings for the P1800 were further pruned to a worthwhile degree before the manufacturing process actually began in earnest.

There was, however, one cost addition made in the process of evaluating build costs for the P1800, and this was in the area of tyres. Originally, cross-ply tyres had been intended to be fitted, but during the 'shake-down' road-test programme, it was found that radials gave a sufficiently significant improvement to the handling and roadhold-ing of the car such as to justify their fitment as standard to the production models. It should be remembered that radial tyres were far from common on new cars of the time, most manufacturers preferring to fit the sig-nificantly lower cost cross-ply types, not just

Chassis tags were different, too. This is the Jensen tag attached to the P1800, though unfortunately, you can't quite read the name 'Jensen Motors' on this one, because of a blemish on the tag.

from the point of view of cost, but also from the standpoint that the radial had not yet proved itself. Michelin at that time was engaged in a hugely expensive campaign to prove the fuel saving and long-life benefits of its 'X' tyre, though this tyre did not have the best reputation at the time for handling characteristics in the wet. A number of British-based tyre makers were after this piece of lucrative business from Volvo and eventually, it was Pirelli, at Burton-on-Trent, which secured it, taking delivery of wheels from Sankey at Wellington and supplying to Jensen complete wheel and tyre assemblies.

Essentially, the P1800 was built up mainly of mechanical components from the Amazon parts bins. The design of the suspension was much the same as the Amazon, though the wheelbase was 20cm shorter and the spring rates were clearly different. The postioning of the Panhard rod on the rear suspension was also differ-

ent, but in principle many parts could be lifted from the Volvo saloon and fitted to the new sports car. And, of course, the engine being used in both models improved the sales potential of both models, just as Porsche's use of the Volkswagen engine had been such an advantage in developing sales in its early career.

In the three-year life of the Jensen contract, some 6,000 cars were built at West Bromwich in the VA/HA series. That was far short of the original production targets, but was a figure tolerated by Volvo because it could see the problems endured by Jensen. You might ask why Volvo failed to step in and censure Pressed Steel for its continuing poor performance in the production of the bodyshells and sundry pressings, but in reality the Swedes realized they were in a very difficult position. If they terminated the contract with Pressed Steel, where were they to relocate the work? They had already investigated several alternatives in mainland Europe, without success. It had made more sense to try to place the contract with a company where overland deliveries could be made, for sea transport increased handling costs and damage risks, but the original view that Pressed Steel could do the work and meet volume targets had been the determinating factor behind the decision. Nobody could have foreseen the quality problems that would arise and even when they became apparent, Volvo felt powerless to do much about it, leaving Jensen very much 'in the frame'.

PLANNING THE TRANSFER TO SWEDEN

The reality of the problem for Volvo in 1963 was that it had endured a three-year run of difficulties with Pressed Steel and Jensen which had had a profound effect on production volumes, and thus sales, which had made the profitability of the project very questionable. Because Volvo realized that Pressed Steel had it 'over a barrel' and because it knew that the management of Pressed Steel was unable to do much about these quality problems, Volvo really had to 'walk the wire' of tense relations with Jensen and standards which fell below its aspirations.

Volvo must have known by the end of the first year that the relationship between Jensen and Pressed Steel was not going to be resolved without drastic changes at the Scottish plant of Pressed Steel. Those changes were not going to be made easily, if at all, because of the running tensions between management and workforce and the likelihood of industrial disputes if stromg management was not imposed, and so the Volvo board knew it had to address the problem for itself. The way to do that was obvious and it was already in the Volvo plan, to expand manufacturing facilities in Sweden and transfer production there at the earliest opportunity.

The transfer of production would not be a simple process, though, for Volvo had to negotiate its way out of the Pressed Steel and Jensen agreements. Part of the problem to be faced was the fact that Pressed Steel had the press tools for the panelwork and was not going to be easily persuaded to let them go elsewhere. Quite apart from that, there was then the problem of shipping heavy plant out of Scotland, perhaps into mainland Europe, running the risk of damage on the way and incurring a substantial cost. And who was to say that Volvo would come out of it any better off? With those facts in hand, together with the knowledge that there still was not anywhere in Germany, Italy or France that Volvo could take the work and meet volume targets, as far as

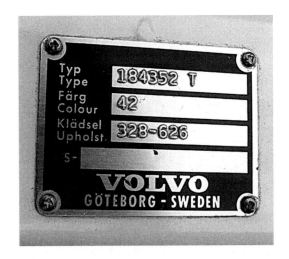

This is the tag attached to the Swedish-built cars after the contract with Jensen had been severed.

Here and opposite are pictures of the 1800s built in Sweden, mixed in with the Duett.

Pressed Steel was concerned, the best approach Volvo could take was to seek to re-negotiate the deal.

As time progressed and Volvo came closer to being able to make space for the production of the 1800 in the old Lundby factory, the problems between Jensen and Pressed Steel were not diminishing, so by late 1962 the decision was made to undertake the switch. Meetings were held with the board of Pressed Steel and the decision was announced that the car would be assembled in Gothenburg from the beginning of April 1963. Pressed Steel would continue to produce the pressings and fabricate the basic bodyshell and then ship it to Sweden for assembly and finishing. On the face of it, it seemed as though, for Pressed Steel, it was 'business as usual', but the job

had only been retained by the most vigorous efforts and Pressed Steel was now clearly 'under the hammer', though for Volvo that position improved with the takeover of the Linwood factory, and the 1800 pressings contract along with it, by the Rootes Group.

As for Jensen, Volvo acknowledged the terrible time the company had endured, having to do so much rectification work before it could begin its own part of the job. Indeed, the problems at West Bromwich had caused considerable difficulties in its own boardroom, for Jensen's principal funding came from outside, in the form of the Norcros Group, and questions were being asked about the costs incurred by the company in doing work that it should not have had to do. There were already tensions in the Jensen

boardroom on other matters, for its own car, the C-V8, which had succeeded the 541, was not reaching production targets either. The only truly stable work in the Jensen factory at that time was the continuing production of the Austin-Healey.

With considerable sympathy for the predicament Jensen had been in from the beginning, Volvo arrived at a compensation package for the West Bromwich firm which included an undisclosed cash sum, reputedly a fairly substantial figure, in consolation for losing the remaining 4,000 cars of that contract. In addition to that, Jensen continued to act in a turnkey capacity for Volvo's component suppliers while also supplying finished components itself. All in all, the deal for Jensen was significantly better than that settled on Pressed Steel, and it has been said

that the West Bromwich firm was compensated to a level where it was better off than it would have been if it had completed the original contract. In addition to that, unbeknown to Volvo at the time, the Jensen board had even contemplated bringing the contract to an end themselves, so Volvo's move was timely and fortunate for them.

THE 1800 COMES HOME

To many in Volvo's Swedish factories, the process of transferring production of the 1800 from Great Britain to Sweden was a logical process of the car 'coming home'. The ultimate plan was for the Swedish-manufactured car to be built at the new Torslanda plant as soon as space became available,

OPPOSITE AND RIGHT :
The 1800S settles down
into production.

The Saint *television series in Britain gave the P1800 a great boost, when the star, Roger Moore (Simon Templar in the series), adopted one as his personal transport.*

though clearly the 121/122 Amazon had priority on floor space in that plant in the beginning. For the time being, the 1800 would have to endure a makeshift arrangement in the old Lundby factory, where the first 1800S cars were to be built.

The designation of the car now changed. No longer was it to be called the P1800 (the 'P' representing 'Personvagn'); instead, it would be simply '1800' with the suffix 'S' to denote the fact that it was now manufactured in Sweden. Whilst this would, in the eyes of many at Volvo, improve the sales potential of the car, it has to be recognized that Jensen had done a great deal behind the scenes to help promote the car worldwide. In 1961, the California State Fair had awarded the P1800 its Gold Medal for outstanding design. The organizers of the Sebring 24 Hours Race had selected the 1800 to be the 'official circuit car' for that event in 1963 and Volvo built on that by securing the same deal for 1964.

The change to production in Sweden was heralded by a number of feature changes. The hubcaps were changed to use the same as those on the Amazon Saloon, with chrome rim trims added to enhance the appearance of the sports car. The front sidelights now incorporated a large orange segment in them to provide coloured direction indicators. A new badge, incorporating the letter 'S' appeared on the tail end of the car and synthetic paint was now used to finish the cars. Inside, detail changes included modified door panels, a 6,500rpm tachometer to replace the earlier 6,000rpm one and upholstery revisions. The engine was now uprated to 108bhp and its top rev limit revised, hence the replacement tachometer. Finish paint colors were now white, red and dark grey – hardly a liberal choice, but the car did seem to sell well despite the limited range of colours.

It seems a little ironic then, that as Volvo was switching production from Great Britain to Sweden, a British television company should give the 1800 its biggest sales boost ever. Even more ironic to reflect now that the television company had to pay full price for the car! What happened was that the producers of the new *The Saint* series had recruited Roger Moore to play Leslie Charteris's character Simon Templar ('S.T.' – 'Saint') and they wanted a suitable car for him to charge around in, chasing villains. Their original choice was the 'E' Type Jaguar, but Jaguar couldn't come up with a car in less than a couple of months (hardly surprising, since the 'E' Type was selling like hot cakes in the United States), and the usual television situation of 'we want a car next week' could not be accommodated.

As a result, the programme's producers went looking for a suitably stylish car and focused on the Volvo P1800. An approach to London's Volvo distributor brought the response that they could buy a car and it could be made available in five days, after registration and pre-delivery checks. Roger Moore was impressed with the appearance of the car, it was thought to be a suitable vehicle to be adorned by beautiful young women and so a white example (what other colour?) was bought and it was introduced to the small screen. Two other factors added to the promotional value of the 1800 in *The Saint* series – firstly, the programme series was exported to the United States, and secondly, Roger Moore, who was a highly thought of 'Mister Clean' icon, bought three in a row for himself (all sporting the stick man and halo emblem of The Saint), so giving the car yet another confidence boost. So, the path to the 1800S's future was laid.

6   Improvements and Establishment in the Key Export Markets

Since long before the introduction of the 1800 sports car series, Volvo had an enviable reputation in the biggest export market of all – the United States of America. The rounded bug-like shape of the PV444 and 544 models had made a mark on the American market and their reliability and durability were highly praised by the hard-using American population, especially in California, where foreign cars were most popular. The market on the Eastern Seaboard was also quite strong, though not as strong, and there was quite a pocket of enthusiasts in the states adjacent to the Great Lakes, especially Wisconsin and Minnesota where the Scandinavian heritage was strong, with many early settlers in those regions coming from the Nordic countries.

Volvo's early market successes in North America were enhanced by its competition successes the world over. For example, the 544 took the first three places in the Little Le Mans Race, a ten-hour endurance event held at Lime Rock in Connecticut, and it led its class in the Pikes Peak Hill Climb in Colorado, quite apart from its performance in Europe in the 2,000-mile Tulip Rally, the Swedish Mobilgas Economy Run and the Royal Swedish Automobile Club's Race to the Midnight Sun. Early advertising in the United States and Canada emphasised the sporting character of the product and the

four North American distributors, Volvo Distributing in New Jersey, Swedish Motor Imports in Texas, Auto Imports in California and Auto Imports (Swedish) Limited in Ontario and British Columbia all supported this philosophy. By the end of the 1950s, Volvo Canada Limited was advertising the 120 as the car that was 'overbuilt' to take it. That same company later employed the very clever advertising line: 'You can drive a Volvo like you hate it for as little as $2,798 – cheaper than psychiatry'. It sold cars and paved the way for Volvo's first real sports car – the 1800.

THE 1800 COMES TO TOWN

Volvo had already established the selling line of promoting longevity. And they had proved it in Europe and America by firstly maintaining production of the 444/544 line-up to 1965, and secondly by demonstrating that the model was an 'eleven-year automobile'. The company had promoted from a very early stage the collection of statistics which ultimately was published by AB Svenska Bilprovning (the Swedish Motor Vehicle Inspection Company) as an annual entitled *Weak Points in Cars*. That publication gave factual and statistical information on

84

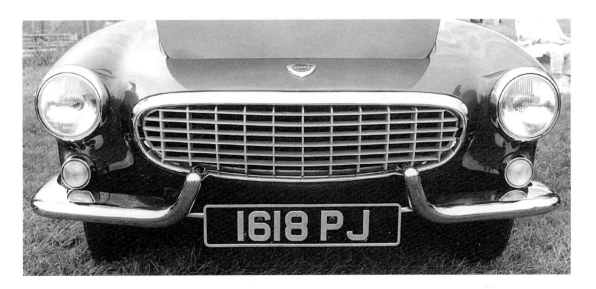

The P1800 front end head on, showing its radiator grille and headlamps.

weaknesses found in a wide range of vehicles and also published data on the median life of cars in Sweden. As a single example, Volvo cars were quoted as having an average life in the early 1960s of 10.7 years, calculated from the number of cars deleted from the Swedish Register.

So, the P1800 was coming into a market place that already had a healthy respect for Volvo as a company and for its products. Bearing in mind also the high sales levels of British sports cars at that time, it was seen as a significant factor that the Volvo P1800 was to be built in Great Britain, especially by a company which had in its own right quite a reputation for the sporting cars of its creation – Jensen. The Jensen 541 was only sold into the United States in very small numbers, but the company's name was also known in sports car circles as the assembler of the Austin-Healey 3000. So Volvo's choice of Jensen was advantageous in terms of promoting the new model against its British and European counterparts.

Logically, the prime competitor for the P1800 in terms of performance and pure good looks was the MGA 1600 coupé. Certainly, the MGA was only a two seater, but, in principle, so was the Volvo, for the two occasional seats were really only suitable for small children, but it was a very pretty car, despite its age, had all the simplicity of the Volvo in mechanical terms and was less expensive. On the other hand, there was the Alfa Romeo Giulietta Sprint coupé, which had more room in the rear for occasional passengers, had that magic twin-cam engine and was in the same price range as the new Volvo. Again, the Alfa Romeo was a little long in the tooth, but it was still a very pretty car. There were all kinds of other sporty cars in the middle, which we shall review in a later chapter.

It was *Road and Track* magazine that described the P1800 as a grand touring car of a type much in the news at a price that many people who could not afford a Ferrari or an Aston Martin would be able to pay. Volvo North America grabbed at that line

*An 1800S by the lakeside. Getting across some of Sweden's country
lanes would have been a good test for the car's ground clearance.*

and capitalized on it, offering the car as
'either the most expensive economy car in
the world, or the least expensive Gran
Turismo car in the world' and going on to
say: 'We'll sell you either one'. 'Either one'
was, of course, one and the same – the Volvo
P1800. This same advertising line was
expanded upon by Volvo, with an advertisement that featured views of three cars head
on – a Ferrari, an Aston Martin and a Volvo
P1800. The key line to the advert was:
'Which one cost $3,995?' The answer was
obvious, but it was a clever development of
the line that this was the least expensive GT
car. Volvo added credibility to that advertisement by saying that both the Ferrari and the
Aston Martin were well worth their price
tags of over $10,000, claiming then that the
P1800 was worth a lot more than its $3,995.

Meanwhile, in Canada, Great Britain
and Australia, the road testers were saying
nothing but good things about the new car.

Canada Track and Traffic magazine
described the P1800 as 'Volvo's caviar addition to its bread-and-butter line of utility-
first cars and trucks.' There were lines like:
'Rough riding reminded us that whatever
Volvo builds stays built.' What a compliment! And it went on. In the road tester's
final paragraph, he wrote: 'At $6,000 this
car would be a bargain. At $3,995 we feel
it's a steal and Volvo will be hard-pressed
to fill the orders.' Of course, Volvo *was*
hard-pressed to fill the orders.

Back on the advertising trail, the
super sports car comparison was expanded further, from the simple direct quota-
tion of Ferrari and Aston Martin prices to
a set of six pictures, illustrating Aston
Martin, BMW, Facel Vega, Ferrari,
Maserati and Mercedes-Benz, with prices
ranging from $10,500 to $12,990, and posing the question 'What's it like to own a
$10,000 car?' The answer came: 'Find out

for $3,995'. If we did not already know, we were reminded that: 'You pay over $10,000 for a Ferrari or an Aston Martin and get this: disc brakes, four-speed synchromesh transmission with optional overdrive, live rear axle, independent front suspension, precise steering, complete instrumentation including tachometer, European styling and coachwork. You pay $3,995 for a Volvo P1800 and get the same.' This advertising was sharp and clever and refreshingly honest. You were told that a P1800 would not do 150mph, which many of the $10,000 cars would, but you would need a race track upon which to do it. The P1800, on the other hand, would do over 100mph, used no more fuel at 90mph than a Volkswagen did at 70mph and all you would need was a stretch of highway to enjoy this kind of performance.

THE 1800 TAKES OFF

In California, the P1800 was well received, as the Gold Medal at the 1961 Trade Fair testified. After some early frustration over orders being paid for and cars not being delivered, California's sporting motoring fraternity began to look closely at the new Volvo when deliveries finally did trickle through. They liked what they saw and the order book began to build steadily. The prime appeal of the P1800 was actually not for the out-and-out sportster, who probably was much more interested in Jensen's other subcontracted product, the Austin-Healey 3000. That was thought to be a full-blooded sporting car, with real competition potential. The Volvo, on the other hand, was recognized as a much more civilized sporty car – no racer, but a thoroughly reliable long-legged touring car with a distinctly sporting flavour.

The Volvo P1800 and its Market Adversaries – 1962					
Car and Model	**Engine Type and Size**	**Gearbox**	**Road-Test Speed**	**Consumption**	**GB Price** (does not include tax)
Volvo P1800 coupé	In-line 4cyl w/cooled 1,780cc	4-sp + o/drive	105.5mph (169km/h)	25–32mpg (11–8.8/100km)	£1,335
Alfa Romeo Giulia Spyder	In-line 4cyl w/c dohc 1,570cc	5-speed	109mph (175km/h)	28–34mpg (10–8/100km)	£1,470
Lotus Elite S/E	In-line 4cyl w/c sohc 1,216	4-speed	120mph (139km/h)	28–35mpg (10–8/100km)	£1,495
MGA 1600 Mk II	In-line 4cyl w/cooled 1,622cc	4-speed	105mph (169km/h)	25–31mpg (11–9/100km)	£663
Porsche 356B 1600S-90 coupé	Flat-4 air/cooled 1,582cc	4-speed	115mph (185km/h)	28–36mpg (10–7.8/100km)	£1,707
Sunbeam Alpine	In-line 4cyl w/cooled 1,592cc	4sp + o/drive	101mph (163km/h)	25–38mpg (11–10/100km)	£712
Triumph TR4	In-line 4cyl w/cooled 1,991cc	4-speed	110mph (177km/k)	25–30mpg (11–9.4/100km)	£825

What's it like to own a $10,000 car?

Find out for $3995.

This is the Volvo P1800. Road & Track magazine put it through its paces and wrote: "The P1800 is a very civilized touring car for people who want to travel rapidly in style, a Gran Turismo car of the type much in the news these days —but at a price that many people who cannot afford a Ferrari or Aston Martin will be able to pay."

You pay over $10,000 for a Ferrari or Aston Martin and get this: disc brakes, 4-speed synchromesh transmission with optional overdrive, live rear axle, independent front suspension, precise steering, complete instrumentation including tachometer, European styling and coach work. You pay $3995* for a Volvo P1800 and get the same.

One thing. A P1800 will not do 150 mph. Many of the $10,000 cars will—all you need is a race track to enjoy this kind of performance. The P1800 will do over 100 mph. At 90 it uses no more gas than a Volkswagen uses at 70—all you need is a highway to enjoy this kind of performance.

*MANUFACTURER'S SUGGESTED RETAIL PRICE EAST AND GULF COAST POE. WEST COAST, $4080.

'The $10,000 dollar car – for $3,995' said Volvo, blatantly parading
its P1800 against the products of such famous sports car makers
as Aston Martin, Ferrari and Maserati.

*The Triumph TR3A Hardtop was, to put it bluntly, crude, but was a
'hairy-chested' sports car. Not for the meek in highly tuned form,
the TR3A stood well against the Volvo 1800, though it was
getting a bit 'long in the tooth'.*

The early cars were not without the odd problems, though nobody in the press had any adverse comments to make about panel fit or finish paint quality. There were comments from customers, which were echoed by road testers, about the low swivel point of the shoulder harness seat belts (not yet inertia reel type), as they clamped down uncomfortably on the shoulder of the driver or front seat passenger when pulled up tight enough to retain the occupant in his or her seat and hold them safely against the risk of impact. Also, there seemed to be some excessive axle tramp in the earliest models and a few odd clunks in the drive line. This was largely cured by a revision of the shock absorbers and changed rubber mountings on the rear axle. By adding a little extra sound deadening material between the rear occasional seat and the luggage compartment, along with the structural modifications, the clunks and rattles disappeared, as did the axle tramp.

Now, it is significant to say, with the knowledge of the tensions and metal finish problems which beset Jensen in the production process, that very few criticisms arose from customers, dealers or journalists about the surface finish or build of the car. One correspondent reported that the P1800 was 'the best car the Jensen brothers had ever made'. Praise indeed, especially when that correspondent went on to report that the panelwork was impeccable and that the

Volvo 1800S Coupé (F, M & P Series) 1965–68

Construction	Pressed steel fabricated and welded box-section sub-chassis with unitary steel coupé bodywork
Engine	Type B18B
Crankcase	Cast Iron crankcase with integral cylinder block
Cylinder head	Cast iron with two valves per cylinder
Cyls/type	Four in-line
Compression	10.1:1
Cooling system	Water, with thermostat & belt-driven water pump and fan
Bore & stroke	84.14 mmx80 mm
Capacity	1,780cc
Main bearings	Plain bearings throughout – five mains
Valves	Two overhead per cylinder, pushrod actuation
Fuel Supply	AC mechanical pump to two SU carburettors
Power output	115bhp @ 5,800rpm
Ignition system	Coil and distributor with single spark plugs
Lubrication	Wet sump with gear driven pump
Brakes	
Type	Disc front and drum rear with hydraulic actuation
Transmission	Volvo four-speed synchromesh plus reverse/Laycock o/drive optional
Clutch type	Single dry plate.
Gear ratios	14.26:1; 9.07:1; 6.20:1; 4.56:1; 3.46:1; Reverse=14.80:1
Final drive ratio	4.56:1 with 0.76:1 overdrive
Suspension/Steering	
Front Suspension	Independent coil with double wishbones, telescopic shock absorbers and anti-roll bar
Rear Suspension	Coil, with trailing arms locating axle in the longitudinal plane and Panhard rod for transverse location
Steering type	Cam/roller steering box with divided unequal length arms
Wheels	Pressed steel 4.5J x 15
Tyres	165–15 Pirelli Cinturato radials
Dimensions	
Wheelbase	2,450mm (96in)
Track (front)	1315mm (51in)
Track (rear)	1315 mm (51in)
Kerb weight	2,496lb (1132kg)
Top Speed	108mph (174kph)

paint finish among the best he had seen, smooth and completely free from 'orange peel'. Apart from a couple of odd chrome spots, the finish was described as 'flawless', demonstrating how well Jensen had dealt with whatever problems the poor welds and panel finish had presented to them.

Why was the Volvo such a success against the competition? First of all, what was the competition? Well, there were the two obvious contenders already mentioned, the MGA 1600 coupé and the Alfa Romeo Giulietta Sprint. There was the Austin-Healey 3000, the Triumph TR3A, the Sunbeam Alpine, all of which

The Volvo P1800S and its Market Adversaries –1964					
Car and Model	Engine Type and Size	Gearbox	Road-Test Speed	Consumption	GB Price (does not include tax)
Volvo 1800S coupé	In-line 4cyl w/cooled 1,780cc	4-sp + o/drive	108mph (174km/h)	25–32mpg (11-8.8/100km)	£1,335
Alfa Romeo Giulia Spider	In-line 4cyl w/c dohc 1,570cc	5-sp syncro	109mph (175km/h)	28–34mpg (10–8/100km)	£1,470
Ford Capri GT	In-line 4cyl w/cooled 1,498cc	4-sp syncro	93mph (150km/h)	28–30mpg (10–9.4/100km)	£728
Lotus Elan 1600	In-line 4cyl w/c dohc 1,558cc	4-sp syncro	115mph (185km/h)	28–35mpg (10–8/100km)	£1,061
MGB GT coupé	In-line 4cyl w/cooled 1,798cc	4-sp syncro	105mph (169km/h)	25–31mpg (11–9/100km)	£855
Porsche 356C coupé	Flat-4 air/cooled 1,582cc	4-sp syncro	115mph (185km/h)	28–36mpg (10–7.8/100km)	£1,668
Triumph TR4	In-line 4cyl w/cooled 1,991cc	4-sp syncro	110mph (177km/k)	25–30mpg (11–9.4/100km)	£825

would need optional extra hardtops to make them weatherproof. The Porsche 356 was a coupé, as was the smaller Lotus Elite, though the Morgan Plus Four was only ever going to be weatherproofed by its hood. Against all of these other makes and models, the P1800 was quiet, comfortable and long-legged. The Alfa Romeo, the MGA, the Porsche, the Sunbeam Alpine (with a hardtop) were all similarly long-legged and compared variously in comfort and handling. The Lotus was purely an enthusiast's car, being somewhat harsh and temperamental, the Morgan was the modern car for a vintage enthusiast. The TR3A and Austin-Healey were more 'hairy-chested' sports cars, though the Healey with a hardtop could be used as a grand tourer, despite slightly harsher suspension than that of the Volvo.

Having compared the P1800 with all these other European sporting cars, it is fair to say that Volvo's ploy of comparing its car with vehicles of much higher specification and price was very effective. It took the Volvo outside its natural competitive group and stood it up against cars of much higher price and specification. This had the desired effect of putting a large gap between the price of the

Volvo and its chosen competitors. Volvo made sure that all the specification items of its car were repeated in the higher priced (and much higher powered and better appointed) cars, so it could say: 'all the features they have, we have' and bingo – the value for money factor is hammered home. The absolute masterpiece of Volvo advertising was the one which described the 1800 as 'sort of a souped-down Ferrari'.

It's sort of a souped-down Ferrari.

The Volvo 1800S will do in fourth what a Ferrari does in third.
About 105 miles an hour.
Which, unless you're insane, is fast enough.
And while the 1800S may not offer you the sheer speed of an expensive GT car, it does offer you the same kind of styling and comfort.
It also offers you something else. The economy and dependability of a Volvo.
In short, the Volvo 1800S is half souped-down Ferrari, half jazzed-up Volvo.
If you can't afford $15,000 for the cream of the GT cars, give us $3,970* and we'll sell you the half and half.

This Volvo US advertisement: 'Souped down Ferrari', was really quite cheeky, but it certainly grabbed attention!

IMPROVING THE BREED AND EXPANDING THE MARKET

Australians who were interested in seeing this new sporty Volvo were, in the meantime, beginning to wonder if it would ever find its way to Antipodean shores, as the car had been on sale for well over a year in the United States before even one of the original press test cars found its way south from Europe after a test programme there and in North America. By the time *Wheels* magazine writer Peter Hall got his hands on the car, it had covered over 14,000 miles (22,526km), most of it hard test driving

Volvo 1800S Coupé (S Series) 1968–69	
Construction	Pressed steel fabricated and welded box-section sub-chassis with unitary steel coupé bodywork
Engine	Type B20B
Crankcase	Cast Iron crankcase with integral cylinder block
Cylinder head	Cast iron with two valves per cylinder
Cyls/type	Four in-line
Compression	9.5:1
Cooling system	Water, with thermostat & belt-driven water pump and fan
Bore & stroke	88.9 mmx80 mm
Capacity	1,986cc
Main bearings	Plain bearings throughout – five mains
Valves	Two overhead per cylinder, pushrod actuation
Fuel Suply	AC mechanical pump to two SU or Zenith-Stromberg carbs
Power output	118bhp @ 5,800rpm
Ignition system	Coil and distributor with single spark plugs
Lubrication	Wet sump with gear driven pump
Brakes	
Type	Disc front and drum rear with hydraulic actuation
Transmission	Volvo four-speed synchromesh plus reverse/Laycock o/drive optional
Clutch type	Single dry plate.
Gear ratios	13.502:1; 8.471:1; 5.762:1; 4.30:1; 3.427:1; Reverse=15.22:1
Final drive ratio	4.30:1 with 0.797:1 overdrive
Suspension/Steering	
Front Suspension	Independent coil with double wishbones, telescopic shock absorbers and anti-roll bar
Rear Suspension	Coil, with trailing arms locating axle in the longitudinal plane and Panhard rod for transverse location
Steering type	Cam/roller steering box with divided unequal length arms
Wheels	Pressed steel 4.5J x 15
Tyres	165–15 Pirelli Cinturato radials
Dimensions	
Wheelbase	2,450mm (96in)
Track (front)	1315mm (51in)
Track (rear)	1315 mm (51in)
Kerb weight	2,576lb (1169kg)
Top Speed	110mph (177kph)

A view inside the P1800, with the rudimentary rear seat backrest in the upright position. You may just be able to discern the Volvo badge impressed into the centre.

The rear panel of the 1800S carried this badge to show you that car was not now the P1800.

Same car, same seat, but this time folded down to provide luggage stowage (following the idea of Porsche's 356 and 911).

and probably the equivalent of over 50,000 miles (80,450km) of normal owner driver usage, and it had barely seen the inside of a workshop or an oil can in any of that time. So Hall was effectively doing a used car test, with a car that was quite well used.

The Australian market had seen Volvos mostly as the result of private imports up to 1961, when Regent Motors in Melbourne and Antill Motors in Sydney took on Volvo dealerships. Peter Antill had made his name in 1929 by driving a Riley Nine from Fremantle in Western Australia to Sydney, covering 2,850 miles (4,585km) in five days and eighteen hours, so he knew what made a tough sporting car. Seeing the 1800, he was convinced that it represented tremendous value at £2,700 (the Australian Dollar had not yet arrived) and Peter Hall's road

test did nothing to dispel that conviction. One of Hall's first impressions of the car was its ability to take him 'over the ton', running at something under 5,000rpm.

The car having covered some rather hard mileage across Europe and the United States, Peter Hall had a good view of both its durability and its ability to hang on to trim and bits of chrome, unlike many other products imported from Europe. Even in its under-serviced and well-used state, the car turned in a very respectable 12.4 seconds for a nought-to-sixty standing start, whilst he was able to achieve over 25 mpg (11/100km). As had been observed by many others before Hall, the car was found to be at its best running at road speeds between 50–100mph (80–160 km/h) on fast highways, mostly floating between direct top and overdrive

This how the 'office' of the 1800S looked.

The standard hubcap of the 1800S changed from the original Swedish hubcap to this one.

top gears. All in all, it was a highly successful and worthwhile road test, with the writer commenting very favourably on the creature comforts (seats, heater and demister and safety belts) of the car. This road test certainly alerted sporty Australians to the qualities of this new car and must have had a greatly beneficial effect on sales there.

In June 1963, Volvo took its most adventurous step yet in the expansion of its market penetration by opening its new Canadian assembly plant in Halifax, Nova Scotia. This enabled Volvo to avoid the punitive import tax which applied to foreign cars brought into the United States. And, of course, it relieved valuable manufacturing space in Sweden for the production of the PV544, the Amazon and the 1800S for domestic and other export markets. By now, the 1800S had become a full-blooded sports car, with the availability of tuning kits that improved performance, and so it was now featuring in the

ABOVE: *A pair of the prototype P1800s, showing from the front view, the upturned 'cowhorn' bumpers and the symbolic 'V' overlaid on the radiator grille, whilst the rear view shows very clearly the exhaust pipes passing through the rear valance and the original position of the fuel filler cap.*

BELOW: *This Volvo publicity shot shows an early West Bromwich-built car on the forecourt of a Swedish filling station. Yes, BP really did do that on their forecourts back then.*

Inside, the back seat centre panel is decorated with this Volvo emblem, resembling the radiator badge (the square badge hadn't yet arrived).

The main instruments of the 1800S, showing how easily they were viewed through the steering wheel.

BELOW: A hedgehog's front end view of the 1800S, showing quite reasonable ground clearance.

ABOVE: Looking down the rear quarter, the line from roof into rear wing is quite clean.

RIGHT: The Scuttle vent of the 1800S.

BELOW: The twin-Stromberg carburettor engine of the 1800S, showing the distinctive air filters, which many people have mistakenly thought were 'add-ons'.

ABOVE: Profile view of the 1800E, showing how little the design changed over the production life of the 1800 Coupé.

RIGHT: This almost-head-on view of the 1800E shows it still to be a pretty car.

YPN 988J

ABOVE: A close-up of the factory-option cast alloy road wheels on the 1800E.

ABOVE: This is the badge that was fitted to the rear quarter panel of the Coupé's top. Note it has the Swedish national colours of blue and yellow in the stripes and a motif of the Swedish crown in gold colour at the top of the little shield which is worked into the letter 'V'.

BELOW: The 'E' engine of the 1800E ('E' stood for 'Einspritz', or 'injection' in Bosch language)

ABOVE: *An on-road view, showing the front quarter of the 1800ES, showing how well it sits on the road.*

LEFT: *Here's the front inside of the yellow 1800E, showing the driver's seat, instrument panel and gear lever. The handbrake's on the other side of the driver's seat.*

ABOVE: The Volvo 1800ES rear valance badging, leaving you under no illusions of what it is you're following.

ABOVE: The large luggage compartment (with the rear seats folded down), revealing the luggage retention straps, holding down the owner's picnic basket. The straps were in fact quite effective at holding down substantially heavier articles, too.

BELOW: The 1800ES on a country lane, showing the elegant rear view of the car.

An 1800S, with factory optional alloy wheels, in an idyllic setting.

SCCA's production racing car championship. This prompted the advertisement with the headline: 'Driving isn't bad for it'. The same ad went on: 'Now just because it's built like a truck, don't get the idea it performs like one. The Volvo 1800S has been the SCCA National Racing Champion for the last two years in the F-Production class.' The advertisement finishes with this amusing statement: 'Which leads us to conclude that the Volvo 1800S is either the world's fastest, prettiest truck, or the world's toughest, most reliable sports car. You can drive either one without being driven to the poorhouse'.

Volvo 1800E Coupé (U and W Series) 1970–72	
Construction	Pressed steel fabricated and welded box-section sub-chassis with unitary steel coupé bodywork
Engine	Type B20E
Crankcase	Cast Iron crankcase with integral cylinder block
Cylinder head	Cast iron with two valves per cylinder
Cyls/type	Four in-line
Compression	8.7:1
Cooling system	Water, with thermostat & belt-driven water pump and fan
Bore & stroke	88.9 mmx80 mm
Capacity	1,986cc
Main bearings	Plain bearings throughout – five mains
Valves	Two overhead per cylinder, pushrod actuation
Fuel Suply	Electric pump to Bosch Jetronic fuel injection system
Power output	135bhp @ 5,800rpm
Ignition system	Coil and distributor with single spark plugs
Lubrication	Wet sump with gear driven pump
Brakes	
Type	Disc front and drum rear with hydraulic actuation
Transmission	Volvo four-speed synchromesh plus reverse/Laycock o/drive optional
Clutch type	Single dry plate.
Gear ratios	13.45:1; 8.56:1; 5.85:1; 4.30:1; 3.43:1; Reverse=15.2:1
Final drive ratio	4.30:1 with 0.797:1 overdrive
Suspension/Steering	
Front Suspension	Independent coil with double wishbones, telescopic shock absorbers and anti-roll bar
Rear Suspension	Coil, with trailing arms locating axle in the longitudinal plane and Panhard rod for transverse location
Steering type	ZF cam/roller steering box with divided unequal length arms
Wheels	Pressed steel 4.5J x 15
Tyres	165–15 Michelin XAS radials
Dimensions	
Wheelbase	2,450mm (96in)
Track (front)	1315mm (51in)
Track (rear)	1315 mm (51in)
Kerb weight	2,560lb (1161kg)
Top Speed	110mph (177kph)

Car and Model	Engine Type and Size	Gearbox	Road-Test Speed	Consumption	GB Price (does not include tax)
The Volvo 1800S and its Market Adversaries – 1968					
Volvo 1800S coupé	In-line 4cyl w/cooled 1,780cc	4-sp + o/drive	108mph (174km/h)	25–32mpg (11-8.8/100km)	£1,335
Alfa Romeo 1750GT Veloce	In-line 4cyl w/c dohc 1,779cc	5-sp syncro	116mph (187km/h)	23–25mpg (12–11/100km)	£1,585
Fiat 124 coupé	In-line 4cyl w/c sohc 1,588cc	4-sp syncro	105mph (169km/h)	25–27mpg (11–10/100km)	£1,480
Lotus Elan +2 coupé	In-line 4cyl w/c dohc 1,558cc	4-sp syncro	125mph (201km/h)	26–28mpg (10.8–10/100km)	£1,554
MGB GT coupé	In-line 4cyl w/cooled 1,798cc	4-sp syncro	105mph (169km/h)	25–31mpg (11–9/100km)	£855
Porsche 912 coupé	Flat-4 air/cooled 1,582cc	4-sp syncro	110mph (177km/h)	28–30mpg (10–9.4/100km)	£1,668
Triumph GT6 coupé	In-line 6cyl w/cooled 1,998cc	4-speed	110mph (177km/k)	26–28mpg (10.8–10/100km)	£879

Whilst a few early modifications were made to the running gear and interior silencing of the P1800 as it was established in the US market, owner experiences brought to Volvo's attention justified further specification revisions. In 1964, the letter 'P' disappeared officially from the designation of the 1800S and the stylized badge on the flanks of the coupé head disappeared, too. At this time, leather facings appeared on the upholstery and the little storage compartment positioned under the back window (originally intended for a first-aid kit) was discontinued.

As the 1800 became more and more international in its sales, so Volvo saw more need for detail changes. Safety was becoming an ever more public international issue and Volvo was already taking a lead in that field in the world of motor cars,

having fitted three-point seat belts into its cars, so it should have come as no surprise that the 1800 acquired straight full-width front bumpers and rubber inserts in both front and rear bumpers to protect against low-speed impact damage. An indirect safety improvement was the modification of the front seats to make them adjustable for height as well as for reach and backrest angle, the safety aspect being that a comfortable driver is a safer driver. By 1965, the seats acquired a lumbar adjustment, whilst the road wheels lost their rim trims, but acquired new hubcaps. An additional minor safey feature added in 1965 was a passenger grab handle, something which many other European sports cars had featured for years.

There were continuing small modifications made to the 1800S to improve its performance and its appearance. On the performance side, for 1966 the engine output was raised to 115bhp, largely by improving exhaust gas flow. This was achieved by the fitment of twin exhaust pipes from the manifold and modified silencers. A closed circuit crankcase ventilation system was introduced at around the same time, so reducing the risk of emission of fumes into the inside of the car. Engine cooling was now also a closed circuit system. The two principal cosmetic changes of 1967 were the chrome strip on the sides of the body, which now ran in a straight line rather than following the moulding line at the rear of the door, and the radiator grille. The new grille employed more horizontal strips, so reducing the 'egg-crate' appearance.

Other detail changes included new door handles, modified licence plate holders and asymmetrical beam headlamps.

TOWARDS A NEW DECADE

As Volvo progressed towards the 1970s, a string of modifications were made that were aimed at keeping the car abreast of its competition. Whilst the 'eleven-year old Volvo' concept continued to be a motivating factor for retaining the model much as it was from the outside, Volvo was clearly aware that it was getting a little 'long in the tooth', as few sports cars managed to remain viable for much longer than seven

The B20 engine of the 1800S, fitted with Stromberg carburetters (not SUs, as you might think at first glance).

*This was the phosphate dip in process at Olofstrom. All Volvo
bodies went through this treatment, though it took some
perfecting on the 1800.*

The 1800E, registered, but sitting at a dockside, perhaps waiting for a ferry. Note the changed radiator grille.

The Volvo 1800E and its Market Adversaries – 1972					
Car and Model	**Engine Type and Size**	**Gearbox**	**Road-Test Speed**	**Consumption**	**GB Price** (does not include tax)
Volvo 1800E coupé	In-line 4cyl w/cooled 1,986cc	4-sp + o/drive	110mph (177km/h)	25–32mpg (11-8.8/100km)	£1,585
Lotus +2S 130	In-line 4cyl w/c dohc 1,558cc	5-sp syncro	125mph (201km/h)	25–27mpg (11–11.5/100km)	£2,124
MGB GT coupé	In-line 4cyl w/cooled 1,798cc	4-sp syncro	105mph (169km/h)	25–31mpg (11–9/100km)	£1,143
Opel Manta Rallye	In-line 4cyl w/cooled 1,897cc	4-sp syncro	103mph (165km/h)	25–27mpg (11–10.5/100km)	£1,194
VW/Porsche 914/4	Flat-4 air/cooled 1,679cc	4-sp syncro	102mph (164km/h)	25–28mpg (11–10/100km)	£1,861
Triumph GT6	In-line 4cyl w/cooled 1,991cc	4-speed	110mph (177km/h)	25–30mpg (11–9.4/100km)	£1,014

*Here, the assembled body is cleaned up after phosphate coating
and prior to paint.*

or eight years. There were signs of declining sales in dealer forecasts by 1967, though that year's ouput matched the 4,500 of the previous trading year. So, the 'P' series cars were announced in August 1967, with a number of minor modifications, including a 'safer' three-spoked steering wheel, a divided steering column that allowed for collapsibility under impact, and 'collision proof' controls for the US market models. Another feature exclusive to the North American market at that time was the introduction of head restraints on the two front seats.

The North American market was very important to Volvo, since almost 30 per cent of its car production was sold there. This meant that the company, already notable as a leader in car safety in its own right, had to take note of American safety and emission legislation and incorporate provisions for that legislation into its cars. These were the days of the famous (or infamous, dependent upon how you saw him) Ralph Nader, an expatriate from the American motor industry who made a name for himself by introducing a whole string of safety and anti-pollution measures aimed, so many people thought, at a dual agenda – that of 'cleaning up America' and making its cars safer to ride in, but also of making it ever more difficult for foreign cars to enter the country. Sadly, much of what he did created a near-perfect platform for the Japanese invasion of the US car market which continues to this day.

In 1968 and 1969, Volvo made quite substantial changes. Firstly, with the advent of the B20 2-litre engine for the 140 series of saloon cars, there was an opportunity to bring more power to the 1800S, whilst being able to comply with US emission standards. With a compression ratio of 9.5:1, another 3bhp was added to the 115 of the earlier B18 engine, as well as a much cleaner exhaust. The clutch and final drive were also modified, whilst new air cleaners were fitted to the carburettors, which could now be either SU or Zenith, dependent upon the market

The full rear end view of the 1800E.

The 1971 'W' Series black plastic radiator grille made the car quite
attractive from the front, in an age when chromed 'egg crates'
were going out of fashion.

destination of the car. A dual brake circuit was another significant safety feature, whilst really the only external mark of change was the B20 badge on the radiator grille, noting that this was now a two-litre 1800, for the model name was not changed.

Also, during the winter of 1968–69, with the expansion of manufacturing facilities in Sweden, Volvo was able finally to break the link with Pressed Steel by shipping the press tools for the 1800 bodies to Olofstrom. After settling down the body production at home, the next step came in August 1969, with the 'T' series model, which had a further improved power unit. Now, Bosch K-Jetronic fuel injection was adopted, partly to improve power, partly to make the engine cleaner, as American emission standards were

tightening. Now, the power output was 135bhp at 6,000rpm and so the gearbox was changed to accommodate the higher torque input. The gearbox was a ZF, made originally for the new 164 six-cylinder-engined saloon and the car became known now as the 1800E ('E' standing for *Einspritz* – fuel injection in German). The dashboard and instruments were also changed, whilst improved interior ventilation was improved by the installation of air outlet grilles on the rear flanks

The 'U' and 'W' series 1800Es continued the line, with further minor modifications in 1970 and 1971. But the most significant option in the history of this sporting car was the introduction of the Borg Warner BW35 three-speed automatic transmission. A potentially new market was opened up, Volvo felt, and the sales figures for the years 1969–70 and 1970–71 seemed to bear that out, because from a low of 1,693 in 1968–1969 (the lowest number of 1800s ever sold in one year, except for the first), sales rose to 2,799 in 1969–1970 and went up to 4,750 in 1970–1971. The two biggest export markets for the 1800 now were the United States and Great Britain, though by far the largest number went across the Atlantic, particularly automatics.

The last changes to the 1800 came in August 1971. Most notable of these was the black plastic radiator grille, above which was now positioned a rectangular badge, featuring the three crowns of Sweden above the original emblem, which was now placed in a square. The road wheels had domed and chrome-plated nuts with a small chrome hubcap, with a letter 'V' on it at the centre, and bright steel rim trims. The non-US models were fitted with the B20E engine of 135bhp, whilst the US models had the B20F power unit, which

produced only 125bhp as a result of all the emission control kit. Glassware was the other feature that benefited from a change, in that tinted glass was now fitted to all windows in the car, much of the benefit of that being aimed at the American buyer, though in Sweden, it also conferred a benefit, in that it reduced glare from winter snows. And that was the end of the road, for the 1800E coupé was discontinued in June 1972.

VARIATIONS ON A THEME

As the P1800 established itself in the world's markets, a number of private coachbuilders took a second look at it and decided that they could improve on or add to its attraction. For example, British coachbuilder Harold Radford designed and built a convertible version of the sporting Volvo. In some ways, it was a more attractive car than the original coupé, as it made

The 1800E rear quarter panel vent, with integral filler cap in the moulding. A tidy piece of styling.

Fissore's design exercise on the 1800, a 'Fastback' which several people took seriously, though it never got into production.

better use of the rear fins than did the line of Pelle Petterson's original design. However, the whole structure of the car was considerably weakened by cutting off the roof, despite the measures taken to restore strength to the body by a series of gussets and steel reinforcements. Nonetheless, the odd example survives to demonstrate the very attractive roadster that Radford built.

Italian coachbuilder Fissore created a fastback GT body on the P1800 in 1963, though when you look closely at the product, there was not a great deal of new coachwork involved. It may be that Fissore had in mind the likely cost of production if his design was adopted by Volvo as an option, but whatever his reasoning, the only real change to the original bodyline was the roof, which had a hint of Ford Mustang about it. Needless to say, the Fissore design was quietly forgotten as Volvo's own design team went to work to produce the odd variation.

One of Volvo's early restyling projects was to revise, as Fissore had done, just the roofline of the P1800. The particular project here was to modify the car into a pure two-seater. The new roof was a more angular concept than the original, with a greater area of glass to create a more 'open' feel to the car from the inside. The result had the appearance of a cross between a Volvo P1800 and a Lancia Fulvia, for the roofline was distinctly Lancia. However, the finished result did not really work, for the angular line of the roof did not blend well with the more curved line of the original car so, like many other design ideas, it was abandoned, although not before a full-scale model had been built to prove or disprove the idea.

Another Volvo creation was its own fastback coupé. Now this design retained in its entirety the front end of the original car, but from the scuttle back, it was a totally new line. Gone were the original rear fins with their chrome cappings, to be

*A variation on the theme – a Volvo 1800S two-seat coupé looking
very much like the Lancia Fulvia coupé of the time.*

*Volvo also produced a GT Fastback on the 1800 and displayed it as
a 'concept' car, but again, it did not reach production, because the
1800ES was just around the corner.*

Volvo 1800E Coupé (T Series) 1969–70

Construction	Pressed steel fabricated and welded box-section sub-chassis with unitary steel coupé bodywork
Engine	Type B20E
Crankcase	Cast Iron crankcase with integral cylinder block
Cylinder head	Cast iron with two valves per cylinder
Cyls/type	Four in-line
Compression	10.5:1
Cooling system	Water, with thermostat & belt-driven water pump and fan
Bore & stroke	88.9 mmx80 mm
Capacity	1,986cc
Main bearings	Plain bearings throughout – five mains
Valves	Two overhead per cylinder, pushrod actuation
Fuel Suply	Electric pump to Bosch Jetronic fuel injection system
Power output	130bhp @ 5,800rpm
Ignition system	Coil and distributor with single spark plugs
Lubrication	Wet sump with gear driven pump
Brakes	
Type	Disc front and drum rear with hydraulic actuation
Transmission	Volvo four-speed synchromesh plus reverse/Laycock o/drive optional
Clutch type	Single dry plate.
Gear ratios	13.502:1; 8.471:1; 5.762:1; 4.30:1; 3.427:1; Reverse=15.22:1
Final drive ratio	4.30:1 with 0.797:1 overdrive
Suspension/Steering	
Front Suspension	Independent coil with double wishbones, telescopic shock absorbers and anti-roll bar
Rear Suspension	Coil, with trailing arms locating axle in the longitudinal plane and Panhard rod for transverse location
Steering type	ZF cam/roller steering box with divided unequal length arms
Wheels	Pressed steel 4.5J x 15
Tyres	165–15 Pirelli Cinturato radials
Dimensions	
Wheelbase	2,450mm (96in)
Track (front)	1315mm (51in)
Track (rear)	1315 mm (51in)
Kerb weight	2,560lb (1161kg)
Top Speed	110mph (177kph)

replaced by a flowing line of roof and rear that would have been a credit to Pininfarina. The roofline, being longer as a 'fastback' coupé style, was able to be held higher over the larger rear seat area to make the car a true two-plus-two coupé. All in all, this design made for quite an attractive car, though it was dropped in favour of another idea for an extended coupé with a hatchback rear opening. That concept was ultimately to develop into a production variant of the 1800S, to be known as the ES.

Before the ES actually came into being, the Volvo design team went on to produce its own ideas for a sporty hatchback.

Several design sketches were made, leading ultimately to the creation of a car known variously as the 'Beach Car', the 'Hunter', the 'Barrel' and the 'Rocket'. These ideas were being put together in the mid-1960s, resulting in the building of an example of the 'Rocket' (or less polite 'Barrel', so nick-named because of the shape of the rear panel). Many people have likened this model to the Reliant Scimitar GTE, but it is quite clear that Volvo had absolutely no way of knowing what Reliant was working on and, perhaps more to the point, had drawn up the 'Hunter', a precursor to the 'Rocket', long before the Reliant hit the streets. It might even be said that the Reliant bore a remarkable resemblance to the Volvo 'Hunter', but with Volvo's tenden-cy to keep things under wraps for as long as possible, the similarities were clearly noth-ing more than coincidence.

During the 1960s, Volvo had struck up a working relationship with a little known Italian designer and coachbuilder called Coggiola. Coggiola had been a Ghia designer before branching out on his own and when he was presented with the sketches and photos of the 'Rocket', he observed that it was likely to be very expensive to retool for the manufacture of this as a variant of the 1800S. In any event, the tail end did not look quite right. It was too heavy for the rest of the car and so Coggiola went to work on adapting the basic 1800 into what was effectively a sporting station wagon, retaining much of the original line, even the rear fins, which now blended much better into the bodyline. Coggiola's cre-ation was grafted on to an 1800S during late 1968 and was to become known as the 1800ES, of which more later.

7 A New Variant –
The 1800ES Hatchback

There are those who would say that Volvo has always been inclined towards the eccentric. Certainly, to build cars designed deliberately to last for eleven years could fairly be considered to be just a little eccentric. And to keep what many people described as a scaled-down version of the '41 Ford in production until 1965 from 1944 – twenty-one years – also seems just a little eccentric. So perhaps we should not have been surprised that the Gothenburg car maker would want to turn a sports coupé into a sports station wagon!

The sporting hatch concept was no new idea even in the mid-1960s, although Volvo was certainly ahead of Reliant in the design stage. Unfortunately, Reliant actually got there first in terms of announcing their GTE, though it was to have little effect on the Volvo's sales potential, as the Volvo's prime market was the United States, where the Reliant simply did not have the reputation or the after-sales support. That first sporting hatch, however, was a very different car, in that it came from Britain's premier sports car maker, Aston Martin, in the form of that company's DB2/4 in 1953. Harold Radford, the coachbuilder who had produced the P1800 convertible, also built a shooting brake (station wagon) conversion on the Aston Martin DB5 not long after that model was announced in 1963.

Developing the theme, Aston Martin went on to produce the DB5 shooting brake some time before the Volvo 1800ES. However, in fairness, it was more of an estate car than the Volvo.

110

EARLY CONCEPTS

One might reasonably conclude that Volvo's earliest ideas about creating an extended hatchback could have come from seeing Aston Martin's Radford Shooting Brake. After all, the idea was fundamentally the same, although the scale was different. Aston Martin was one of the world's top sports car makers and the idea of creating a shooting brake seemed to appeal to a very small number of people who 'had everything' and wanted a car of distinction in which to be seen at country functions. Only twelve Radford conversions were built, the first being DB5/1411/R, built in 1964. They certainly were elite motor cars and the idea clearly appealed to other car makers, including Volvo.

It was during that time when coachbuilders were taking a look at the Volvo P1800 as a prospect for a revamp that the Gothenburg design team, led by Jan Wilsgaard, thought of experimenting with their creation. The hatchback idea occurred to them and they began work on designing a possible Volvo hatchback. This was in the mid-1960s and that first design exercise was to be known as the 'Beach Car'. Using the P1800 as the basis of this sporting station wagon, the new design extended the rear end, perhaps a little too far to maintain equal proportions, but raised the roofline, blended in the rear flanks and introduced the hatch. The roof had a short lip at its rear end, whilst the tailgate sloped forward from the bottom, much along the line of the later Reliant Scimitar design.

The design line of the Beach Car was quite attractive, although the original sketches seemed to make the hatch disproportionately large. This is probably in part due to the fact that the hatch was a large glass area. The practicality of that large glazed panel was that it gave a wide, clear view for the reversing driver, often a criticism of sporting coupés. On presentation of the design to the Volvo board, it was felt that perhaps a more adventurous design was needed to expand interest in Volvo's sporting model and so, despite the clean lines, the design was shelved. Now it was back to the drawing board.

Next off the design table came the 'Hunter'. This was actually thought by many to be a less attractive design, as it was shorter and rounder than the Beach Car. The only part of the original vehicle retained in the design sketches for this new model was the front end. Again, a large glass rear panel was a feature of the design, but the side windows seemed quite small. Even the door glazing appeared to be of a smaller area than that of the original P1800, as the bottom line rose up from the rear of the door to meet the shallow rear quarter light. It had the impression of making the body look more chunky than it really was, although the clay model was more convincing. The other plus factor for the Hunter was that it was estimated that it would be quite inexpensive to manufacture, in that it used major components of the original body structure, and being basically a re-roof job, so it went to the prototype stage.

In addition to the Hunter, there was the 'Rocket', sometimes uncharitably referred to as the 'Barrel', because an end-on view of the rear had the distinct appearance of a beer keg, though to be fair, seen from a high angle of view, it did not look quite so odd. Anticipating American legislation in the area of impact resistance, the rear bumper had a substantial rubber insert and was wrapped round the bodywork from the bottom, surrounding and protecting the rear light clusters in the process.. Within the rear end design also, the original rear wing

This was Volvo's 'Beach Car', designed in the process of reaching the 1800ES.

The Hunter was another design project along the route to the ES...

(or fender) line was abandoned, the whole being faired into the new smooth panel line.

Again, a prototype of the 'Rocket' was built, but before that, a full sized clay model was made in which the two sides were not identical. As far back as the doors, both sides of the model were the same, but then the rear quarters became distinctly different. The left side retained the upturned moulding towards the rear of the door, which then followed a flared line up into the rear flank. The rear window followed the roof line at its upper edge, but the bottom edge followed a gentle curve up to the rear end, leaving quite a short space

...and the 'Rocket' was yet another variation on the sportwagon quest.

from top to bottom. The rear edge of the side window was a couple of inches from the inner edge of the tailgate aperture.

The right-hand side of the 'Rocket' model was a much more attractive sight, with its smooth sides and rear window shaped very much like that of a Porsche 911. This meant that the side window ended about 12in (30cm) from the tailgate opening. It allowed a clear area of side panel to accommodate the fuel filler cap without it looking odd and made the proportions of the whole rear quarter look right. The least elegant part of the whole original design was the tailgate itself, as it was quite heavily framed, no doubt to provide a vertical line that corresponded with the bumper on the lower half. The glass itself was recessed into the tailgate, providing a lip all the way round it. The clay model was examined and from the conclusions drawn, the prototype went into build.

By the time the 'Rocket' went into build in the metal, a number of minor styling changes had been made. The side window selected was the right-hand-side design, though modified a little to deepen the bottom line of it, which actually had a detrimental effect on the finished appearance, as it was less symmetrical. The tailgate

still had quite a deep frame, although the recess for the glass was reduced, making the rear end look a little cleaner. But then the Volvo management team raised the question: 'Was this new design a little too advanced for the Volvo buying public, or even for the market at large?' It had to be remembered that Volvo was not in the forefront of car styling and most would-be Volvo buyers looked for more conservative design lines. As a result, the 'Rocket' project was shelved and the Italian designer/coachbuilder Sergio Coggiola was called to the rescue.

THE CONCEPTS OF CARROZZERIA COGGIOLA

Carrozzeria Coggiola was formed when its principal left the employ of Ghia to set up on his own. His initial activity was to produce design prototypes for other carrozzerie under subcontract. However, it was not long before the company set up its own design department and undertook such original creative work as was called for by Volvo with the 1800S. Sergio Coggiola had established a working relationship with Volvo in the early days of the

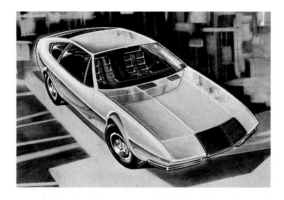

While Coggiola was adapting Volvo's own original design to sportwagon configuration, they were also working on a design of their own on the 1800 floorpan and this is the result in sketch form. It was called the 'Viking'.

1800, shortly after Ghia had submitted designs for the creation that went to Pelle Petterson. Having abandoned the fastback 1800S coupé design, the 'Beach Car', the 'Hunter' and the 'Rocket', Coggiola was now brought in to examine the 1800 and exercise his own design talents on the car.

Coggiola was given an 1800S to go to work on after examining what others had

done, reviewing the original car and concluding that his design would make the minimum of alterations to the basic shape. It was clear that Coggiola had looked closely at the 'Rocket', especially at the Kamm tail effect of the abrupt end of the car which had some of the characteristics of Ferrari's 'Breadvan' racing coupé. He was determined not to repeat it. Instead, Coggiola simply extended the roof line of the 1800 from its highest point in an almost straight line from front to rear. The original door shape was retained below the glassware, though the top edge of both door and its glass were straightened out to follow the line along to the rear pillar.

The tailgate was, for its time, a very adventurous design idea, for the creator used a piece of shaped glass that had no frame to it at all. The hinges, top mounted, were actually bolted into the glass itself. The gas-filled struts were also anchored at their outer ends to the glass, with their ball joints secured through it. And the handle at the bottom of the tailgate was also bolted through the glass. Around the edge of the glass, extending from one hinge to the other, was a slender trim, primarily aimed at ensuring that the

And here's the 'Viking' in the metal at the Turin Motor Show, looking quite like a Ferrari 308GTB4 or a Lamborghini Jarama.

The definitive prototype 1800ES in the workshops of
Carrozzeria Coggiola during its construction.

glass itself did not get chipped and that the owner did not cut a hand or suffer any other injury whilst raising or lowering the tailgate. It was a clever design which ensured the maximum possible extent of rear view and prevented the tailgate from looking ungainly or excessively heavy.

The prototype was built in Coggiola's workshops in late 1968. There is a photograph of it in the final phase of preparation, with windows masked for paint, taken in December 1968. But despite the fact that this design was virtually the definitive object, the ultimate vehicle did not go into production until 1971, which is what allowed the Reliant Scimitar to go on sale and be acclaimed as the first-ever production sporting station wagon. The earlier Aston Martin hatchback DB2/4 and the DB5 shooting brake could not be described as 'production' in the true sense of that word. On the other hand, the Volvo 1800ES, as it was to be labelled, did become a production car. Unusually, there were no noticeable revisions in the transition from the prototype to the production model.

Demonstrating the flexibility of Carrozzeria Coggiola, in 1971, as the 1800ES was going into production, the design for a new car on the 1800 floorpan came from that design office. A profile illustration of the car, finished in a bronze colour, truly illustrated the talent of Sergio Coggiola, for this was a well-proportioned and stylish car that could easily have gone into production for Volvo and would almost certainly have won a new market for the company in the sporting car world, to say nothing of winning back old customers, many of whom were now looking for replacements for their earlier 1800s.

Unlike many design exercises carried out by the leading carrozzerie, this one was far from outrageous. The watercolour design profile of the Coggiola design was taken further, with a prototype car being displayed at the Paris Salon in October 1971. It attracted a great deal of media and public attention and was dubbed the 'Viking' – not the most imaginative name for a car that certainly *was*. Looking back today, it bore a striking resemblance to

When the first 'leaks' about the 1800ES came out, many assumed
the design to be a 'crib' of Reliant's GTE, both in idea and outline.
Nothing could be further from the truth, for the concept was
twenty years old already and the Volvo actually had a cleaner
and more attractive outline than the Reliant.

The 1800ES in a most practical application – on the beach.

Ferrari's 308GTB4, which appeared two years later, also at the Paris Salon, and took the market by storm. Why then, you may ask, did the Volvo have the same effect? The answer is very simple. Firstly, Volvo was not announcing this new design as the next 1800S, though many members of the public walked away with the impression that this was exactly what it was. But there was also some confusion, because alongside the Coggiola 1800ESC was the production 1800ES, so the public was left asking whether or not this new design was an addition to the range, available alongside the 1800E and 1800ES. Of course it was neither – it was just a design exercise, but one which told Volvo, if it had been listening, that this could have been the way ahead for their sports car.

DEVELOPING THE 1800ES

The 1800E coupé was joined then, in 1971, by the 1800ES, which quickly found itself being compared with the Reliant Scimitar GTE. This was really quite an unfair comparison,

The engine room of the 'E' and 'ES' models, now a fuel injected two-litre.

not least because Volvo had the idea first and the Reliant could fairly be described as more of a 'kit' car, in that it borrowed all of its mechanicals from other sources. The design of the Reliant was very pleasing, albeit remarkably close in line to Volvo's earlier Beach Car (that similarity could really only ever have been purely accidental, as it was highly unlikely that Reliant, even if they could have achieved it, would have cribbed the Volvo design). There were two factors in the design and construction of the Reliant which did not help it against the Volvo. The

The Volvo 1800ES and its Market Adversaries – 1972					
Car and Model	Engine Type and Size	Gearbox	Road-Test Speed	Consumption	GB Price (does not include tax)
Volvo 1800E sportswagon	In-line 4cyl w/cooled 1,986cc	4-sp + o/drive	110mph (177km/h)	25–32mpg (11-8.8/100km)	£2,120
Ford Capri 3000E	V-6 w/cooled 2,994 cc	4-sp syncro	114mph (183km/h)	23–27mpg (12-10.5/100km)	£1,347
MGB GT coupé	In-line 4cyl w/cooled 1,798cc	4-sp syncro	105mph (169km/h)	25–31mpg (11–9/100km)	£1,143
Reliant Scimitar GTE	V-6 w/cooled 2,994 cc	4-sp syncro	120mph (193km/h)	22–28mpg (12.9–10/100km)	£1,924

first was its glass-fibre body, which many people were apprehensive about on the grounds of safety as they feared that the car would disintegrate around them in a collision. The other factor was the frontal aspect of the Scimitar. Its radiator grille did not come up to the rest of the design – it was vague and undistinctive, whereas the Volvo radiator was the car's positive identity.

In December 1971, one of Britain's leading motoring magazines, *The Autocar*, presented its first impressions of the new 1800ES. Several of the features of the original P1800 that had been abandoned were now revived for the ES. For example, map pockets appeared on the door panels and whilst a glove compartment in the dash was still not available, a small lockable box appeared between the seats for those things you did not want to leave in view – provided they were not too big, that is. One feature that was much improved, except for the sense of claustrophobia, was the rear occasional passenger compartment. The hard seats were made a little more comfortable and the backrests were improved; legroom was still very restricted, although headroom was naturally better as a conse-

quence of the raised roofline. Another feature which was a distinct improvement was the carpeted luggage compartment, the carpeting running up the back of the rear bench seat backrest. This meant that when the seat was folded flat, the whole space from behind the front seats was a quite large, albeit shallow, fully carpeted luggage area, the forerunner of carpeted trunks in production cars generally.

The car was considered to be of very high quality build and interior fit, but *The Autocar* was of the opinion that interior and road noise were excessive. The driving position was thought to be a bit cramped for tall drivers, which seems a little odd, as many Swedes are quite tall. The biggest criticism was headroom. From the driver's seat, the instrumentation was much improved, with individual round black dials, printed with white characters, all mounted on a wood veneer finish. The steering wheel was still a plastic-rimmed large affair which did not exactly fit into the style of the time, when smaller, leather-rimmed wheels were the fashion. The writer commented favourably on the heated rear window/tailgate and observed that there were several small

The tailgate of the 1800ES – impressive, as it was unframed glass.

The Volvo 1800ES and its Market Adversaries – 1973					
Car and Model	Engine Type and Size	Gearbox	Road-Test Speed	Consumption	GB Price (does not include tax)
Volvo 1800E sportswagon	In-line 4cyl w/cooled 1,986cc	4-sp + o/drive	112mph (180km/h)	25–32mpg (11-8.8/100km)	£2,120
BMW 2002 touring	In-line w/c sohc 1,997cc	4/5 syncro	118mph (190km/h)	29–32mpg (9.8–8.8/100km)	£2,349
MGB GT coupé	In-line 4cyl w/cooled 1,798cc	4-sp syncro	105mph (169km/h)	25–31mpg (11–9/100km)	£1,570
Reliant Scimitar GTE	V-6 w/cooled 2,994 cc	4-sp syncro	120mph (193km/h)	22–28mpg (12.9–10/100km)	£2,398

recesses under the rear floor for the stowage of odds and ends. All in all, the ES had scored well, though there was some surprise that the heater was not more efficient and the heavy steering was a carry-over from the original coupé.

The Americans received the new Volvo with great enthusiasm, and coined the definition 'Sportwagon' into the bargain. *Car and Driver* conducted a humorous examination of the car, painting a picture of future Middle America that, in hindsight, came remarkably close to the truth of things. This was the car that would solve every American young blood's motoring problems. The author observed that the Corvette and E-Type were out, with their luggage space limited to the ability to carry 'two slices of whole wheat toast'. The young driver of that time (January 1972) needed a car that would be compatible with other toys of the age, like golf clubs; the weekend luggage; an outboard motor and a couple of gallon cans of fuel; picks, pitons and rope enough to climb Mount McKinley or even all the kit you need for a weekend's motor sport at Watkins Glen or Monterey.

Styling of the 1800 coupé was thought by this reviewer to have best benefited

from being scrapped in favour of something new, but good old Volvo was continuing with the eleven-year car philosophy. That said, the *Car and Driver* writer was of the opinion that by stretching the 1800 into a station wagon, Volvo technicians had done with the 1800 what should have been done all along. They had now brought their car right up to date in terms of customer needs and produced a 'sporty' car, instead of an out and out sports car. Road noise was picked up, as it had been at *Autocar*, and the steering was criticized as being a little imprecise and heavy. But at the end of the day, *Car and Driver's* observation: 'Maybe what GM needs is an intravenous injection of Volvo courage' said it all!

The other leading American journal, *Road & Track*, endorsed much of what *Car and Driver* had said about the Volvo 1800ES, going on to observe that it was the Volvo which would put the sportwagon concept on the US map. *Road & Track's* conclusion was that Volvo had succesfullymade the transformation, producing the first sportwagon big enough to serve as one that could be bought in America and had done such a nice job of the aesthetics that the car was a real

The interior of the 1800ES, showing the Connolly hide leather seats...

...and the inside of the rear compartment with the back seats folded down. Quite a load space, although not quite big enough to lie down in.

head-turner. The sting in the tail was that the writer suggested it had been done on a car that should have been replaced rather than reworked – it was a good solid car, but a crude and old-fashioned one. However, taking the edge off the comment, it was 'one of a kind'. *Road & Track* did not think that Volvo would have any trouble selling the 1800ES.

APPROACHING THE END OF THE LINE

Even Volvo knew that its sporty creation could not go on for ever, neither in coupé or sportwagon form. So it really came as no surprise in the market place at large when the coupé version of the 1800 was dropped from the Volvo range in June 1972. The last 1800E to be built came off the line on 22 June 1972. The 'Y' series of the 1800 was only offered in 1800ES form, from Chassis

The front quarter of a late 1800ES.

Number 3070. Immediately obvious modifications included a greater sweep to the windscreen wiper blades, whilst the ratio of first gear had been changed. Invisible changes, but valuable ones from the occupants' safety point of view, were the inclusion of side impact bars inside the doors and the decision to make all the interior fittings and furnishings fire-resistant. Volvo's safety philosophy was finding its way into the 1800ES, just as in all its other models. The author can verify the tremendous value of the side impact bars in a Volvo, a 144 in this instance – when driving round a gentle bend at about 30mph, an improperly closed passenger door flew open, struck a lamp post and slammed itself shut. The damage was a dent in the door which, surprisingly in any other car no doubt, was perfectly capable of being opened and closed normally immediately after the incident. Fortunately, there were no other cars nearby, nor any other occupants in the Volvo, but it was a convincing demonstration.

It was as much the changes needed to the US market models that brought Volvo to the conclusion that the time had arrived to discontinue the 1800ES. The B20F engine fitted to the last version produced only 112bhp, a reduction of 23bhp from the best option previously available, just to accommodate 91-octane lead-free fuels. Impact-resistant bumpers for the 1973 model year increased the length of the car and were beginning to look like oversized examples inadvertently taken from a different and much larger car. In total, 8,077 1800ES models had been built. Over 78 per cent of 1800s built between 1970 and 1973 had been exported to the United States and Canada, whilst just over 1,000 of all variants found their way into Great Britain, the second largest export market. Only a few hundred remained in Sweden by the time Volvo decided the time had come to draw a line under the 1800. On 27 June 1973, 1800ES Chassis Number 8077 rolled out of the factory.

8 Handling the Competition

When the P1800 was first announced, it was to join a market already very well supplied with sports cars from Britain and Europe. Many of them were designed in the same format as the Volvo, that is to say front engine and rear-wheel drive, using a pushrod overhead valve power unit. Others had more sophisticated engines, with single or twin overhead camshafts, with engine and gearbox in unit, either at the front or rear, but all with drive at the rear. So why would Volvo want to launch a sporting car into a market place already filled with cars that carried names far better known for their sporting heritage? Well, not least because it was firmly believed throughout the world's motor industry that sports cars sold other products.

Volvo never really took the sports car market seriously in the same way as so many other manufacturers. It had no sporting car tradition in the way of Alfa Romeo, Austin-Healey, Lotus, MG, Porsche or Triumph – all of which companies had built enviable competition records over many years. Volvo certainly had a record of competitive success, but with its production saloons, like the PV444 and PV544, in events such as rallies, rather than out-and-out racing. But it had its reputation for making solid, reliable cars of high build quality, and it was upon this that it based its claim to be able to make a sports car capable of competing in the market.

THE TARGET MARKET FOR VOLVO

Volvo had a wealth of engineering experience upon which to draw in the process of building its second sports car, remembering that its first, the P1900, was not a commercial success. The motive, as has already been said, was to produce a sporting car that would act as a talisman for the Volvo name. Sporty cars sold other cars, and it was the other cars that Volvo wanted to sell in volume. The company's post-war reputation had been built on Europe's perception of the mid-sized family car, a category described in modern American terms as 'compact'. Volvo had already launched, very successfully, the PV444 into North America, its biggest target market area, and it had been used in hill climbs, rallies and reliability trials with some notable success. Volvo had produced the 'sport' engine to considerable acclaim, but had failed with its first sports car attempt, partly probably because of the decision to use glass fibre as the body material in a market that was not quite ready for it, although Chevrolet, with much more cash behind the launch, had managed it with the Corvette.

Knowing they had a 1.8-litre engine on the way helped the Volvo design team and the board of directors who would have to approve the expenditure, to focus on the size of power unit for this new vehicle. The decision to use Pelle Petterson's body design was right for them, in that it was different and would have appeal to the American market, although styling tastes change and this one almost lost out because of the crippling delays in getting it into production. The decision to use an Italian styling house was right, because it added credibility to the concept, as did the choice of Jensen Motors to assemble the production car. Now, all that had to be decided was the range of competitors against which the new P1800 was to be pitted.

Initially, the competitors foreseen were the MGA, the Triumph TR3A, the Sunbeam Alpine, the Alfa Romeo Giulietta Sprint and the Porsche 356. All had their own cult followings, but it was not the hardline sporting competitor or dedicated one-make enthusiast that Volvo was seeking to win over. It was the motorist who wanted a 'sporty', rather than an out-and-out 'sports' car – the person who wanted a car to make a statement, whilst having a car of good performance potential. It was lower end of the 'grand tourer' market that Volvo decided to seek out as the prime target for its new car, building on the existing success of the 85bhp sports engine.

Given that there were misgivings about the durability of the P1800's styling, it being quite late going into production, the fact of that delay in some ways worked in Volvo's favour. For example, the 1600cc sports cars already in the market were joined by Alfa Romeo's Giulia, 1600 successor to the Giulietta, whilst the T-6-bodied Porsche 356B 1600 had also joined the fray. These two leading competitors had also raised their prices, making the Volvo look better value for money. The high chrome-capped fins of America's giants were gone now, but there was a sector of the market that regretted their passing and the Volvo's hind quarters were a reminder of something lost, without being as outrageous as some of

those American cars had been. That Volvo never intended to build enough cars to flood the market anyway was an advantage, as the P1800 would build into a cult car, as had earlier Volvos.

Volvo already knew that its sole key to expansion and ultimate survival was export and the biggest export market available was the United States. Great Britain had also proved to be a receptive market for Volvo, not least because of the level of reciprocal business being transacted between Swedish and British companies in all kinds of activities. Furthermore, Sweden was a key member of EFTA, the European Free Trade Association, which had been formed in 1959 as a competitive organization to the European Economic Community. A great deal of reciprocal trading in manufactured goods had already taken place and it was very much to Sweden's benefit, which had nothing like the manufacturing infrastructure that existed in Great Britain. The P1800 was in the forefront of EFTA's early growth, making it much less expensive to take the presswork and assembly of the car to Britain than to a country like France or Germany, though Karmann was tipped to be the front runner for the P1800 at one time.

Having established that the United States would probably account for around 75 per cent of the 1800's production, the determination of the car's position in the market was really preordained. The specific competitors to the Volvo would be: the Alfa Romeo Giulia Sprint coupé; the Fiat 124 Spider with hardtop; the MGA 1600 coupé; the Porsche 356B coupé; the Sunbeam Alpine hardtop; and the Triumph TR3A hardtop. There was nothing available from US manufacturers, although Datsun's SP311 sports car would become an outside contender from Japan. So, the die was cast and it was for Volvo now to do what it could. It had already made some inroads into the US market with the announcement of the P1800 in 1961, when many customers placed orders and paid in advance – a technique which would be exploited in later years by some of the world's leading sports car makers.

THE CHALLENGE FROM MILAN

Alfa Romeo had an enviable reputation in the United States as a sports car maker of substance, although opinions about the car's durability differed between the East Coast and California. This was because, in a large part of Europe and on the East Coast of America, weather conditions were much more generally humid, regardless of temper-

ature – ideal conditions for rust and Alfas rusted with the best of them. But on the West Coast, where the weather was generally drier, cars did not rust so much, if at all (how many cars are being reimported to Europe today with the tag 'California car', implying they are rust-free?), and so the only problem with Alfa Romeos located there was to maintain them and keep them running smoothly.

By 1961, the Alfa Romeo Giulietta was in its last year as a 1,300cc, as customers were beginning to look for more power, so Alfa Romeo, like many other manufacturers, decided to fit a bigger engine. The FIA (Federation Internationale des Automobiles) had raised the capacity limit of Class F from 1,500cc to 1,600cc and so the way was clear for the Milanese manufactur-

The Alfa Romeo Giulia Sprint 1750 appeared over a decade after the first Giulietta, yet retained much of the original lines and style of its predecessor.

er to increase the engine size from 1,290cc to 1,570cc, changing the name of the car to Giulia on the way. Not much else was different, except the price, and so this was to be Volvo's first, albeit more expensive than most, adversary. It would be a hard act to match head on, for the Alfa Romeo was a grand touring coupé in every way.

With the reputation that Alfa Romeo brought with it from its great catalogue of racing successes, in both long-distance sports car and Grand Prix events, it was hardly surprising that the engine of this small car was of aluminium alloy construction and featured five main bearings. In roadholding and steering response, the Alfa was clearly ahead of the Volvo, whilst the Italian scored better on fuel consumption too, with almost five more miles to the Imperial gallon (eight pints of twenty fluid ounces, whereas the US gallon consists of eight pints of sixteen fluid ounces each). Internally, the Alfa Romeo was better equipped than the Volvo, with better sound deadening and carpeting, though the instrumentation was similar.

Out on the road by 1962, the Giulia Sprint was a pretty remarkable drive, which is what you would expect from a company which had fielded Giuliettas in every international sports racing event since 1953, including Le Mans and the Mille Miglia. Turning in a top speed of 107.5mph (173km/h) on 92bhp at 6,200rpm, the car was still basically the Giulietta with a 1600 engine, but by 1963 it had acquired an updated body, in the form of a scaled-down version of the Bertone 2600 and an uprated engine to improve its maximum by another 5mph (8km/h). It was a truly beautiful sporting two-plus-two, with a particular following of its own, but at a price. To the dedicated 'Alfista', there was no contest between the Giulia and the Volvo P1800, but to the casual newcomer who was looking at a European sports touring car for his or her next purchase, then the Volvo stood a chance.

FIRST THE ELITE, THEN THE ELAN

Alfa Romeo had shown the way to many a sports car maker, in proving that a well-designed engine of smaller capacity could do the job of many a car with a larger power unit. So it should have been no surprise when a small firm from Hornsey, in London's East End, engineered a lightweight two-seat coupé with a displacement of only 1,216cc, to compete against the 'big boys'. The company was, of course, Lotus Engineering Limited (as Lotus was then known) and the car was the Lotus Type 14, better known as the Elite coupé, powered by a Coventry Climax 1,216cc single overhead camshaft engine known as the FWE type. The engine was an adaptation of the 1,100cc FWA, the change in last character of model designation being used to denote the increase in the bore to 76.2mm.

The Lotus Elite came into being from Colin Chapman's conviction that he could produce a car to run in the under-1,300cc Grand Touring Class and compete with the best of them – the best at that time being mainly Alfa Romeo, with the Giulietta Sprint coupé. The Elite was offered in complete form or as a home assembly kit, primarily as a means of putting a serious sports car into the hands of less than affluent owners. It was a tactic which would mark future Lotus success. Unlike any of its predecessors, the Elite was of glass-fibre construction, using many aircraft techniques. The light weight was a very important element in the success potential of this little car, though Lotus's design and development team, under John Frayling's supervision and guidance, were also well aware that if this new car was to succeed as a production sports car, it had to be one which people could get into and out of easily. That they were successful is demonstrated by the degree of reverence held today by motoring enthusiasts for the Lotus Elite. In competition, it established an enviable reputation for itself in the hands of such names as Peter Lumsden, Les Leston (who hasn't heard of DAD 10?) and many others.

The Elan came along in 1963, succeeding the Elite. It had a larger engine, a Cosworth-Ford 1,600cc, but slightly lower maximum speed, as the Elan was intended to be a little more street-refined. It had a better appointed interior, too, although it was still only a two-seater, even in coupé form. Like the Elite, the Elan had a fibreglass body too. The logic of the decision was that fibreglass would withstand much more severe impacts without damage than aluminium, which would dent very easily, and that fibreglass could be moulded to any shape required. Furthermore, where reinforcement was needed, metal plates could be moulded in, sandwiched between layers of glass matting and bonded with the resin bond used to seal the laminates together.

The Lotus models were fantastic revelations in the world of sports cars. Race-bred, they proved able to out-corner and out-pace

The Lotus Elite was a small two-seat coupé of tremendous appeal and very graceful lines. Despite its engine being only just more than half the size of the Volvo 1800, it could outperform the Volvo in almost any situation. But it was sold in kit form and was not the most comfortable of cars at speed.

The Lotus Elan +2S was a magnificently styled, perfectly proportioned grand tourer. This really was a GT car, offering comfort with performance. It was lighter, faster and quite expensive, but bore comparison with the Volvo 1800.

many cars of much higher price and specification. The Elite's nought-to-sixty time was only 11.2 seconds – a pretty respectable time for the 1990s, leave alone 1961, the year of the Volvo's introduction. To make the car even more tractable, it was offered with two SU carburettors as an option, which did nothing for the car's top speed, but helped it along in the intermediate gears. A standing quarter-mile was covered in 18.4 seconds (thirty years later, the Porsche 3.2-litre Speedster only made the distance in 15.85 seconds!).

TWO FROM ABINGDON – THE MGA AND MGB

At the time that the Volvo P1800 was announced and put on sale, the MGA 1600 was in its final phase, as the MGB had been created as its successor and was well advanced towards production. Volvo's mar-keting research had confirmed that sales of the MGA were beginning to fall in the United States, although the coupé version had never sold in large numbers anyway, but it was what was available just at the point of the P1800's release into that market. Whilst the MGA was a superb little sports car, economically priced and endowed with quite a healthy turn of performance (105mph (169km/h), 0–60mph in 12.8 seconds, 25–31mpg (11–9/100km),the coupé version was a little claustrophobic and the car generally was beginning to be regarded as dated. True MG buffs would, of course, continue to buy the 'A' for as long as it was available, but they were not enough in number to keep it alive and so the 'B' took its place in 1963, but only as a roadster, for the MGB GT was a little way off yet.

The one thing which continued to mitigate in favour of the MGA coupé for as long as it was available was its no-nonsense value-for-money image. Its reputation, its

MG Car Company's MGA 1600 Coupé Mk II was a superb quantity-produced car. It might not have had the legs of the Volvo 1800 on a tour, but the 1600 Coupé was snug (perhaps a little close-fitting) and had performance and roadholding to match any Volvo 1800.

turn of speed, its price, and its general level of appointment were good reasons for people to continue buying it. Volvo's case was a more up-to-date design, a bigger engine, an occasional two rear seats and more of a future than the MGA, with quite a bit of British industry in there to help it along. Of course, Abingdon finally succumbed and brought in a successor that had an engine of similar size to the Volvo, was of unitary construction and a more contemporary style. But it was only a roadster and so allowed a gap in its market that Volvo in North America quickly exploited. Weather-proofing and other creature comforts with which the MGB roadster was not endowed won ground for Gothenburg.

It was to be 1965 before the MGB GT arrived on the scene and only 524 of them left the line in that year. Now the roadster could not really have been described as a pretty car, being much more slab-like than its very elegant, and highly acclaimed, predecessor. But the GT, when it arrived, proved to be a thoroughly well-thought-out design, bringing the rear hatch that

Aston Martin had introduced several years before back into currency. If Volvo had not already been producing the sketches which led to the Beach Car design, it might have been said that the MGB GT gave some inspiration to what finally became the Volvo 1800ES – and it may well have promoted a few thoughts on the theme. The new MG coupé was a two-plus-two, with a fold-down rear seat that had about the same amount of rear passenger legroom as the Volvo, but which, by virtue of that fold-down rear seat, gave a little more luggage space than the P1800 in an overall shorter car and with a glazed rear hatch for access.

The 'B' series BMC engine which powered the MGA had been enlarged and developed for use in the MGB and was now of 1,789cc displacement. The gearbox in the MGB was four-speed, like the Volvo, but unlike the Volvo, the optional overdrive was available on third and top gears, instead of just on top. The MG's power unit was endowed with only 95bhp, but that was adequate to propel the

Many said that the MGB GT Coupé was a worthy successor to the MGA, but this author did not hold that view. The MGB was more square, perhaps a little roomier and perhaps a bit faster, but all in all, it lacked the character of the MGA.

cleaner coupé along at 103mph (166km/h), with a fuel consumption of around 25 to 27 mpg (11–10.5/100km). The MG was a harder ride than the Volvo, however, and so the American buyer who was not really looking for a 'hairy' sports car might well fall for the charms of the Volvo in preference.

THE PRODUCT OF ZUFFENHAUSEN

The Porsche 356B 1600 was, of course, rear-engined with the already firmly established and highly-respected flat-four which had its origins in the 1,100cc Volkswagen power unit designed by Professor Ferdinand Porsche for the 'People's Car' of the 1930s. Porsche's design studio was also responsible for creating the mighty Auto-Union Grand Prix cars which helped to elevate Germany to racing supremacy in that same decade.

Because of Britain's punitive taxation policy of the time, the price of the Porsche range, already quite high, was almost doubled by the combination of import duty and purchase tax, especially as the purchase tax was added to the price of the car plus all its costs and after the addition of the import duty, so the duty, which was already a tax in its own right, was taxed again! In 1961, the Porsche 356B 1600 coupé cost around £2,000 delivered, not much more than the Volvo – though it was a very different car, built with different objectives from the pride of Gothenburg.

The flat-four Porsche engine came in two forms the standard unit with pushrod valve actuation and the overhead cam quad-cam type which, of course, was much more powerful, creating a true 100mph-plus vehicle, but at a quite staggering price for a steel-bodied production vehicle, albeit one of quite a specification. The pushrod engine was of 1,582cc dis-

*Porsche's 356B 1600 Coupé, with what was known as the T5 body,
was a very attractive coupé, with lots of luggage space, though not
as much elbow room for its two main occupants as they might
have liked. But it was a very expensive car, even compared
with the Volvo 1800.*

placement, with a bore of 82.5mm, a stroke of 74mm and a compression ratio of 8.5:1, whilst the quad-cam boasted an extra 5.5cc, having a larger bore, at 87.5mm, and a shorter stroke, of 66mm, to give 1,587.5cc on a compression ratio of 9.8:1. In the car, the pushrod unit, at 75bhp, had a comparable performance with the P1800 on the road, top speed being roughly the same, though the Volvo proved more predictable in its handling. On the other hand, the quad-cam Porsche, the GS Carrera, was an out-and-out performance car and not a comparison for the Volvo in any way.

The Porsche was certainly an exciting car to drive. However, it had drum brakes all round (albeit very efficient ones), whilst the Volvo offered discs on the front, a significant step forward in the eyes of many ordinary motorists. On the road, the 356B 1600 showed 101.25 mph (163km/h), whilst its nought-to-sixty time fell two seconds short of the Volvo's figure, at only 14.4 seconds. Fuel consumption was quite good, averaging 27-32 mpg (10.5–8.8/100km), with 28mpg (10/100km) being averaged over one particular 785-mile (1,263km) road test. So, the only real advantage of the Porsche 356B 1600 over the Volvo coupé was its style, which was entirely a matter of individual taste. But it would take the quad-cam-engined Carrera to provide a hint of that neck-snapping performance with which all Porsches became generally associated.

THE SPORTWAGON FROM TAMWORTH

From a little factory straddling the old A5 London-to-Holyhead road (named in Roman times Watling Street), in a small town called Tamworth, emerged the only early challenger to the Volvo 1800ES. The name of the company occupying that factory was Reliant, a firm more famous for perpetuating the three-wheeled car than for making any kind of sports car. The car was one which, oddly enough, went through the same kind of transformation, from coupé to sporting station wagon, as

did the 1800. The coupé was called the Scimitar, the metamorphosis was called the Scimitar GTE (grand touring estate) and it was designed by a man named David Ogle, a car designer of some repute. Reliant felt that their Scimitar coupé was not quite hitting the mark and that something was needed to turn the situation round, or the car would have to be abandoned.

David Ogle's design studio was brought in and given a free hand to redesign in any direction they wanted to, so long as what was designed could to be manufactured with reasonable ease and had mar-

The Reliant Scimitar GTE was not truly an adversary for the Volvo 1800ES, though many people thought the Volvo idea was 'cribbed' from Reliant. If you look carefully at the development line of the Volvo, you will see that it was clearly not a 'crib'.

ket appeal. Clearly, Mr Ogle's design team leader, Tom Karen, studied such cars as the MGB GT and the products of European design houses, which were in the habit of producing 'concept' cars, and then he went to his drawing board. At this point one has to ask: 'Did anyone from Ogle Design have a chance to see the Volvo Beach Car in the mid-1960s?' The answer must be that it was highly unlikely, for Volvo had a very tight mantle of secrecy over all its research and development activity and it would have been very difficult for anyone to break through that mantle. But the question is prompted by the remarkable similarity between the two cars in profile.

In real terms, the Scimitar was not a direct competitor to the Volvo 1800ES, in that its body was made from glass fibre, mounted on to a separate steel chassis, and the engine was a Ford V-6 of either 2.5 or 3 litres displacement. Whilst Reliant claimed a 120mph (193km/h) top speed and 25 mpg (11/100km) fuel consumption, contemporary press observations reckoned the fuel consumption was more likely to be in the region of 22mpg (12.8/100km). The price of the Reliant was a little under £1,900 in 1969, whereas the Volvo 1800S coupé was marginally under £2,000 in late 1968, the year in which the Scimitar GTE was announced. By 1972, the situation had reversed, with the Scimitar costing just under £2,400, whilst the 1800ES was priced at a fraction over £2,000. Bearing in mind the markets at which the two products were aimed, there was actually little real competition between them, except perhaps in Great Britain. And even then, Reliant had the market's resistance to glass fibre to overcome, for many motorists were still mistrustful of that material's ability to withstand serious

accident damage. So the 1800ES continued to sell, virtually unchallenged, though in diminishing numbers due to its dated design.

A COVENTRY CHALLENGER – THE SUNBEAM ALPINE

Britain's Rootes Group, anxious to 'climb on the bandwagon' of popular sports cars, and hungry for export currency, especially dollars, decided to expand on a theme it had begun in 1953, producing a two-seater called the 'Alpine'. The original 1953 car had been a sort-of sporting two-seat version of the Sunbeam Talbot '90' Saloon, but not a particularly sparkling performer. The new 'Alpine', on the other hand, was a sporty little vehicle with lines that had more than a passing resemblance to the original Ford Thunderbird. The radiator grille, the raised rear fins, everything about the styling of this car seemed to say 'scaled-down Thunderbird'. Taking a leaf out of Alfa Romeo's book, it had wind-up side windows instead of sidescreens. That, of course, added to the weight, but added to the market appeal in North America, too, thought Rootes. It was certainly a pretty little car, though the later versions were more attractive, and it sold quite well in the American market at which it was unashamedly aimed.

Like the Volvo P1800, the Alpine was really a sporting tourer, with the result that not many became racers, though a few were used in rallies. Weather-proofing on the Alpine with the detachable hardtop was excellent. The hardtop was, like the car itself, a bit Fairlane-ish, though mercifully, it did not carry the 'port-hole' of the American car's hardtop. With a live rear axle, leaf rear springs and coil independent

A very pretty car in its day was the Sunbeam Alpine Hardtop.
Many said it was a 'ladies car', meaning it was rather tame, but the
Holbay engine was capable of making the car match many of its
competitors in performance and it was a good rally car.

front suspension, the car followed custom and practice in the volume sports car market. The three-bearing 1,592cc engine came from the Rapier Saloon, as did the floorpan (though shortened on the way). Wheelbase was 7.2in (18.3cm) and the car weighed just over 2,280 lb (1,034kg) kerb weight. The engine produced a claimed 90 bhp and was 'over-square' by design, with a bore of 81.5mm and a stroke of 76.2mm. Compression ratio was 9.1:1 and maximum power came in at 5,000rpm. A four-speed gearbox was standard, though, as with the Volvo, Laycock overdrive was offered as an option and a Borg Warner automatic came as an option. Bearing in mind the weight of the car, it had a reasonable nought-to-sixty time, at 13.6 seconds, and whilst it was said to be a 100mph (160km/h) car, in standard form, it really only turned in around 95mph (153km/h).

By 1961, Thomas Harrington, a Sussex coachbuilder with a reputation for building long-distance buses, not sporting cars, produced a thoroughly attractive two-plus-two coupé conversion on the basic Alpine two-seater and, whilst expensive, it was quite a striking car which, with overdrive on board, made it a true 100 plus mph motor. The original Harrington Alpine Le Mans, as it was named, sold in moderate numbers to North America, but then, when Rootes announced the Mark IV Alpine, it updated the Harrington and that really was a truly elegant small grand tourer, with well over 100mph available on the right kind of road. The company sold all it could build, but sadly did not build enough, as Harringtons realized that this was not where its future lay and abandoned the project.

The Ryton-produced Mark IV Alpine was quite a stylish little car, with the tail

The Sunbeam Harrington Alpine was the ultimate in Alpine design.
Built by the coachbuilders, Thomas Harrington, it was not made in
large numbers and is now very sought after. This one, a Mark III,
is seen at Sebring in Florida, mixing it with the Porsches.

fins reduced to more acceptable proportions and minor line refinements which gave it an elegance that was widely appreciated. The hardtop was revised to fit the newer line, too, giving the car all the creature comforts of a small saloon, combined with something very close to the performance of a sports car. With a quoted speed of 20.2mph (32.5kn/h) per 1,000rpm in overdrive top and a maximum engine speed in top of around 5,500rpm, the car was now endowed with a true potential top speed of over 110mph (180km/h), its handling and roadholding being quite well matched to that performance. Priced between the MGA and the Triumph TR3, the Alpine developed its own market and certainly gave its parents quite a few much-needed dollars, but it did not really threaten the Volvo 1800.

PRIDE OF COVENTRY – THE TRIUMPH TR3A AND TR4

The Triumph TR3A was an out-and-out sports car, but long-legged enough to be a grand tourer, too. When fitted with a hardtop, it was reasonably snug but, being a fairly noisy car to begin with, the drumming inside the closed area must have been quite trying on a long journey. Styling of the Coventry-built car was different from that of the P1800, in that it was a snubnosed, slab-sided open two seater. The hardtop was an optional extra and though it was quite weather-proof, it had the disadvantage of sidescreens with sliding windows. However, the squarish rear end of the Triumph meant that it had a similar-sized luggage compartment, with one distinct advantage over the Volvo and many of its competitors – external access to the spare wheel, which was withdrawn by removing the panel on to which the rear number plate was mounted. This revealed the spare wheel sitting snugly in its own compartment beneath the boot floor, so eliminating the need to remove luggage in the event of it being needed to replace a flat on the road.

The cockpit area of the TR3A was, however, a bit cramped, with no spare hiproom, though the seats were of a better shape than the P1800 to keep the occupants in place. Driving the car led one to suppose that it was heavier than in fact it was, though it was no lightweight. Close to a ton, it turned in a better nought-to-sixty time than the Volvo at 10.8 seconds, and a higher top speed at 105mph (169km/h) – a genuine 'ton-up' sports car. This was achieved at a quite modest engine speed, 5,250rpm, as the car ran at 20mph (32km/h) in top gear at 1,000rpm engine speed. Power output from the 1991cc Standard Vanguard engine was a true 100bhp, which went a long way towards making the TR3A a quite exciting sports car. There was no heater as part of its standard equipment, though overdrive was available on the four-speed Standard gearbox, priced at £75.

Fuel consumption was another interesting feature, one which perhaps justified the Triumph's larger, 12.5-gallon (57-litres), fuel tank. At low road speeds (though who wanted to drive a sports car at low speeds?) for example, at a steady 30mph (48km/h), the TR3 came home at 43.5 mpg (6.5/100km). At 40mph (64km/h), it went down to 41.5mpg (6.8/100km) whilst at 50mph (80km/h), it went to 38mpg (7.5/100km). But at high cruise speeds, the TR3A could only manage between 24 and 28mpg, whilst the Volvo did about the same.

By the middle 1960s, Triumph had replaced the TR3A with the completely new TR4. Completely new on the outside, that is, for the TR4 used most of the running gear components of the 3A, except for the rack and pinion steering and an enlarged engine to 2138cc. The TR4 retained the live rear axle of the TR3A, though with slightly softer springs to allow for the higher weight of the new car. The Michelotti body made the Triumph an attractive sports car, which sold well in the United States and, when it was available, in Britain and Europe, too. With a maximum of 110mph (177km/h) and 25–30 mpg (11–9.4/100km), it was a popular two-seater, although the space to the rear of the seats was miniscule (an optional seat squab was available for anybody brave enough to ride in the back). The hardtop was novel, in that it featured a 'Surrey' top, a removable roof panel, for refined open-air motoring. The TR4A brought with it independent suspension everywhere but North America, where dealers did not feel that the added maintenance cost was worth the effort.

135

*Logical successor to the TR3 was the Triumph TR4 hardtop. Again,
a two-seater with an add-on, the TR4 was at least a little more
comfortable than its predecessor.*

Triumph, the 'Pride of Coventry', like MG, provided a small gap between the TR3A and the TR4, which Volvo used to its advantage. Like the MG, the Triumph was a car with its own following and was more of an out-and-out sports car than the Volvo. But the Volvo was now establishing its own market slot as a grand touring coupé and was, in the process, opening the door to markets for its other products. The plan had worked.

9 In the Eyes of the Press

The press has always shown an interest in new cars, especially new sporting cars, whether they be 'sporty' or 'sports' cars. The particular attraction to the press of the Swedish Volvo P985 was the fact that it was to be largely manufactured in Great Britain. The new EFTA had been established and reciprocal trade had begun almost immediately between the countries of Scandinavia and Great Britain – indeed, some Scandinavian companies already had established associations, and even registered companies, in Great Britain long before the advent of EFTA. This new Volvo car was one of the first manifestations of that Association and, of course, the press was interested in it for that reason, too.

Volvo's target market for this car was, from the beginning, the United States, with a very long-placed second being Great Britain and, whilst the company had plans to manufacture in North America, Canada was the intended location for that activity. However, with the links between Great Britain and Canada, via the Commonwealth, and Great Britain and Sweden through EFTA, Volvo's plan for a worldwide market was at the beginning of its route to success.

The Autocar *cutaway drawing of the P1800, produced very shortly after the car's announcement.*

FIRST CARS OFF
THE LINE

The American magazine *Motor Trend* was one of the first publications to give mention to the Volvo P1800, when it announced in its byline that the new Swedish coupé would be produced in England. It talked of the design being Italian, by Frua, which is, of course, not quite right, as the basic design and outline of the car came from the board of yacht designer Pelle Petterson, though Frua built the prototypes and contributed something to the refinement of the car's line before it reached production. Quite correctly, the writer tells us that the line of this new beauty from Sweden bore more than a passing resemblance to some of the coupés which appeared on Ferrari chassis during the mid-1950s – certainly the front end of the car was very Ferrari-ish.

The announcement continues with a description of the construction of the new car, the engine which was to power it, the four-speed gearbox with optional overdrive and the large front disc brakes. Since it was common in those days for sports cars to have independent front suspension and conventional semi-elliptic allied to a live rear axle, no fault was found here with that same concept being applied to the Volvo. It would appear, though, that this was where *Motor Trend* stopped listening to the the revelation about this new Volvo, for it went on to say that Pressed Steel Limited in England were to make the bodies (but Pressed Steel had not yet moved it all to Castle Bromwich and Linwood certainly was not in Warwickshire, as any Scot will hasten to tell you) and assemble the cars. Somebody had either forgotten to tell them, or they simply had missed the key point, that in fact it was Jensen in West Bromwich who were to do the assembly job.

It was interesting to note that *Motor Trend* thought the dashboard of the P1800 could have come straight out of Detroit, for that was an observation made by some later reviewers, who were not so taken with that fact. Apart from this, the car generally impressed the American writer and whilst he had not yet had an opportunity to drive it, he did comment that if it handled nearly as well as the PV544, it would be a first-rate grand touring car. The price was noted as being somewhere between $3,000 and $4,000 which, of course, it was, though the final selling price of $3,995 was a bit close to the mark!

In Great Britain, *The Autocar* was one of the first to get more than a passing look at the new creation from Gothenburg and it correctly noted the construction of the car. *The Autocar* made mention of the fact that the new car shared parts with the Amazon saloon, though the body of the P1800 was clearly completely new. The review outlined the fact that the passenger compartment was of conventional concept, with a heavily ribbed floorpan, boxed-in side sills and enclosed top-hat section members extending forward in chassis style to carry the engine and gearbox.

A very strong endorsement comes from this reviewer for the fact that assembly of the car was to be carried out by Jensen Motors, making reference to the company's quite long experience in this area with the British Motor Corporation in the process of building up the big Austin-Healey sports cars, starting with the 100/4 and progressing to the 3000. *The Autocar* felt comfortable with the fact that the small West Bromwich firm, which had a fine reputation for the cars of its own design as well as for subcontract work, would produce this new venture from Sweden, going on to say: 'It is a compliment to British industry that Volvo, who have carefully built up an enviable reputation for quality and attention to detail, should entrust the production of what is their luxury model to British hands'.

In November 1961, the now-extinct British magazine *Sporting Motorist* took a look at the P1800, observing, as had a number of other journals, that a full twelve months since the announcement of the car it was still a rarity on European roads. This was explained by the statement that Volvo had a policy of placing the first cars of any new model on to the Swedish market so as to iron out any bugs before hitting world markets. This may well have been true in part, but the real reason for the long delay in the car's appearance on sale was the string of labour disputes across the British motor industry and no reference was made this.

Once the reporter had arrived in Gothenburg, he was greeted with the opportunity to do a a few hours driving. While not a full road test, at least the writer had the chance of assessing the comfort level and the basic handling characteristics of the P1800. The reporter was struck with the perceived robustness of the car, the comfort and retention of the seats, though a little apprehensive about the limited headroom for taller occupants. Perhaps a little surprisingly, this reviewer took the view that the skimpy rear seats would carry two adults over a journey of reasonable length in sufficient comfort to be at ease. There were not too many people who would agree with that comment, thinking the space far more suitable to accommodating a couple of smallish suitcases.

Out on the road, our reporter was impressed, driving the car along an autoroute, and feeling totally at ease with the instruments and the rather flashy steering wheel. With a high kerb weight of over 2,500 lbs, he felt the car was stable

and the engine tough enough to drag it along to an indicated 170km/h (just over 105mph). Even at high speeds, the car was found to be stable and responsive, with just a little understeer. The review ended with a series of favourable comments, about the handling, the functional qualities of the body, especially the spacious luggage compartment, and the shape. It rounded off with the sentence: 'Altogether, the P1800 appears to be a car well worth waiting for, for it has an unusual combination of speed, good handling, roominess and a robustness of construction which should ensure a lengthy and reliable ownership.' All this from just a few hours with the car.

THE P1800 TAKES TO THE ROAD – TEST

In November 1961, John Christy of *Sports Car Graphic* in the United States, took a P1800 out on a true road test. He opened his review of this sporty Swede with the comments:

> There are some cars that, while utterly delightful, give one the feeling that they should never be taken more than a hundred miles or so from home base. There are others, equally delightful, that make one feel they could be driven around the world with little more in the way of service than replenishing the fuel tank and an occasional change of oil. Sitting firmly on the top of this latter category is Volvo's long-awaited confection, the P1800 GT coupé.

Pretty strong words about a car from a firm that had no real reputation in the manufacture of sports cars and a very substantial endorsement of Volvo's policy of making safe vehicles.

Christy went on: 'With this solidity comes a degree of passenger and driver comfort on the road, at virtually any speed

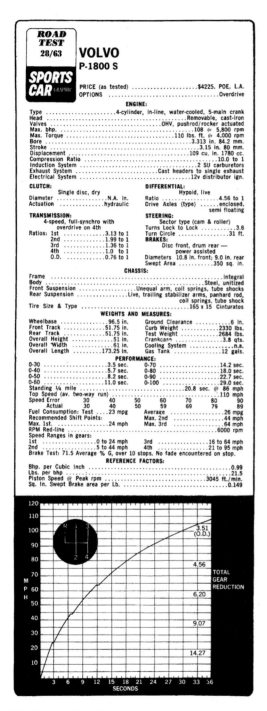

ROAD TEST 28/63	VOLVO P-1800 S

SPORTS CAR GRAPHIC

PRICE (as tested) ....$4225. POE, L.A.
OPTIONS ....Overdrive

ENGINE:
Type ....4-cylinder, in-line, water-cooled, 5-main crank
Head ....Removable, cast-iron
Valves ....OHV, pushrod/rocker actuated
Max. bhp. ....108 @ 5,800 rpm
Max. Torque ....110 lbs. ft. @ 4,000 rpm
Bore ....3.313 in. 84.2 mm.
Stroke ....3.15 in. 80 mm.
Displacement ....109 cu. in. 1780 cc.
Compression Ratio ....10.0 to 1
Induction System ....2 SU carburetors
Exhaust System ....Cast headers to single exhaust
Electrical System ....12v distributor ign.

CLUTCH:
Single disc, dry
Diameter .................................N.A. in.
Actuation ....hydraulic

DIFFERENTIAL:
Hypoid, live
Ratio ....4.56 to 1
Drive Axles (type) ....enclosed, semi floating

TRANSMISSION:
4-speed, full-synchro with overdrive on 4th
Ratios: 1st ....3.13 to 1
2nd ....1.99 to 1
3rd ....1.36 to 1
4th ....1.0 to 1
O.D. ....0.76 to 1

STEERING:
Sector type (cam & roller)
Turns Lock to Lock 3.6
Turn Circle ....31 ft.

BRAKES:
Disc front, drum rear — power assisted
Diameters 10.8 in. front; 9.0 in. rear
Swept Area ....350 sq. in.

CHASSIS:
Frame ....Integral
Body ....Steel, unitized
Front Suspension ....Unequal arm, coil springs, tube shocks
Rear Suspension ....Live, trailing stabilizer arms, panhard rod, coil springs, tube shock
Tire Size & Type ....165 x 15 Cinturatos

WEIGHTS AND MEASURES:
Wheelbase ....96.5 in.
Front Track ....51.75 in.
Rear Track ....51.75 in.
Overall Height ....51 in.
Overall Width ....61 in.
Overall Length ....173.25 in.
Ground Clearance ....6 in.
Curb Weight ....2330 lbs.
Test Weight ....2684 lbs.
Crankcase ....3.8 qts.
Cooling System ....n.a.
Gas Tank ....12 gals.

PERFORMANCE:
0-30 ....3.5 sec.
0-40 ....5.7 sec.
0-50 ....8.2 sec.
0-60 ....11.0 sec.
Standing ¼ mile ....20.8 sec. @ 86 mph
Top Speed (av. two-way run) ....110 mph
0-70 ....14.2 sec.
0-80 ....18.0 sec.
0-90 ....22.7 sec.
0-100 ....29.0 sec.

Speed Error   30   40   50   60   70   80   90
Actual   30   40   50   59   69   79   89

Fuel Consumption: Test ....23 mpg   Average ....26 mpg
Recommended Shift Points: Max. 2nd ....44 mph
Max. 1st ....24 mph   Max. 3rd ....64 mph
RPM Red-line ....6000 rpm
Speed Ranges in gears:
1st ....0 to 24 mph   3rd ....16 to 64 mph
2nd ....5 to 44 mph   4th ....21 to 95 mph
Brake Test: 71.5 Average % G, over 10 stops. No fade encountered on stop.

REFERENCE FACTORS:
Bhp. per Cubic Inch 0.99
Lbs. per bhp 21.5
Piston Speed @ Peak rpm ....3045 ft./min.
Sq. In. Swept Brake area per Lb. 0.149

[Graph: MPH vs SECONDS, with gear reduction values 3.51 (O.D.), 4.56, 6.20, 9.07, 14.27, labeled TOTAL GEAR REDUCTION]

The Sports Car Graphic *road-test data table for the P1800.*

over any reasonable surface, that is almost beyond belief.' He illustrated his point by relating the tale of how a secretary, a pretty knowledgeable lady in the world of motor cars, went along for a ride during the test programme. She made a few odd comments about the appointments of the car and about the sense of stillness experienced in the car whilst moving along at no mean pace. She decided, we are told, to note the comments of the driver and other passenger (implying that she was sitting in the back during this journey), and so she pulled out a shorthand pad and began scribbling away in neat, undisturbed rows of notes, making the comment, after a few miles of this: 'It's as easy as writing in an aeroplane!'

Whilst the car showed itself to be naturally prone to mild understeer (a comment made by most reviewers and road testers of the P1800), it was observed that oversteer could be provoked quite easily, simply by driving the car into a tight corner in second gear and hard throttle. It was possible to overdo it on the road, but only when the driver became over-exuberant. On the track at Riverside Raceway, it was a different scene, for here the driver could really 'have a go', without the fear of traffic travelling in the opposite direction causing problems. Here, the tremendous braking power of the car, combined with the almost equally tremendous adhesion of the Pirelli Cinturatos fitted (inflated to 32 lb per square inch), meant that the driver could realistically drive almost flat out into any corner and emerge on virtually any line he chose, leaving braking to the absolute last.

John Christy's report was not without the odd criticism, though. For example, whilst he was at pains to point out that he was not personally an 'elbow hanger', the driver who was would find this car not too friendly to the 'hold down the door with your elbow' technique. To begin with, the window ledge was a bit too high to do that with any degree of comfort. Secondly, the quarter light post was set a little too far back for comfortable elbow hanging and added to that, the window outer seal apparently had a rather sharp edge to it, which made for discomfort when pressed against an exposed elbow. If that helped drivers stick to the 'ten-to-two' hand position on the steering wheel, then it was no bad thing, for this was not a car to drive sloppily – if you wanted to do that, then a Chevrolet Impala was your car, not a P1800.

On the pure performance front, Christy was clearly impressed. Nought-to-sixty time, for example, was a mere 12.1 seconds, better than many sports cars of somewhat larger dimensions and certainly the equal of the car's leading competitors. The standing quarter mile was almost two seconds slower than the MGA 1600 and nearly three behind the Porsche 356 1600 Super 75. But then it was a heavier car and once moving beyond sixty, it was becoming a little sluggish. That was partly because Volvo, in designing the cam profiles for the engine, wanted this to be more of a long-legged grand tourer than an out-and-out speed machine. The ability to cruise at reasonably high speed for prolonged periods was more important in Volvo's design book than a capacity to outpace the best from Alfa Romeo, MG, Porsche or Triumph.

Back in Britain, Motor magazine was able to road-test the P1800 by August 1962. Its review opened with the criticisms, though all were relevant and none were aiming just to take the car to pieces for the sake of it. The review opens with the comment that the car was strikingly individual in appearance on the outside, but that it conveyed an unexpectedly old-fashioned impression as soon as its occupants sat

inside it. The tester seemed not to like the near vertical position of the steering wheel, the high sides and scuttle line or the rake of the windscreen, which seemed to put the sun visors too close to the foreheads of the occupants. He went on to question the merits of the occasional rear passenger seats which, in his view, were better just left to carrying luggage, for a backseat passenger of even average height would find the limited headroom too restrictive, to say nothing of legroom.

It was not all doom and gloom though, for the report goes on to say that if most of the features outlined recalled the sports saloon of twenty-five years before, then the consolation was that they were combined with a modern fascia, slim windscreen pillars that did not obstruct vision, generous elbow room, a good fresh-air heating system (when the heaters in most British cars were still optional extras), an all-synchromesh gearbox (Porsche was the only other manufacturer that offered the same facility on all forward gears) and in-built safety harnesses – three-point mounted shoulder and lap-type seat belts with all-metal fixings. Seat belts were, of course, considered a peculiarly Swedish thing not to be taken too seriously anywhere else in the world. Attitudes have changed somewhat since those days, but who would have thought it then?

Motor found a few different things about the Volvo P1800 to attract it than did many other testers elsewhere in the world. It was especially impressed with the large doors, allowing easy entry and exit to and from the car. There was a comment about the likelihood of passengers complaining about the seat not being sufficiently curved across the back panel to hold the occupant in comfort, but then logically the writer leaps to the rescue of Volvo by suggesting that the manufacturer considered that the seat belts should be worn at all times and at such a level of tightness as to secure the occupant into the seat to minimize the effects of lateral forces. The fascia was thought to be clean and crisp, easy to read, with switches being at the driver's fingertips, though the smaller instruments – the clock, oil pressure gauge and fuel gauge – were all too small to see at a glance. Performance, on the other hand, was highly praised, with similar findings to those of *Sports Car Graphic* – but amazingly, 32 mpg (9/100km) fuel consumption!

APPROACHING MID-LIFE

We go to Australia for the next road-test review, the first of a group of tests carried out as the car approached its mid-life. The magazine was *Modern Motor*, the tester Barry Cooke and the date was April 1966. The car had now been on the market for five years, almost half its lifetime, if the eleven-year average was to be accepted as the life expectancy of the P1800, which had now changed to 1800S as part of the evolution process. Also part of the evolution process was the improved seating, deeper and better-shaped front seats and deeper upholstery to the occasional rear seat (still cramped, but less numbing on the anatomy). The vented wheels, modified radiator grille and rubber bumper inserts were also part of that same evolution. The seats had an adjustable lumbar support and generally, whilst the driving position was considered low and visibility limited (to the extent of the driver not being able to judge the extremities of the car for a day or two), Barry Cooke was impressed with most of the revised 1800, although not with what he saw as the 'stylistic' dashboard.

Driving the car was clearly a pleasure to this tester, who managed to coax it to 60mph in twelve seconds dead. He record-ed a best speed of 108 mph (174km/h), with a 105mph (169km/h) flying quarter mile. Better yet, Mr Cooke screwed the standing quarter mile down to a pretty remarkable 18.2 seconds, equalling the Porsche 356 Super 75's time, though that car had now gone and had been succeeded by the 356SC and better still, by 1966, the Porsche 912, both of which returned only fractionally better times. During the test, an airline pilot observed to Barry Cooke that he wished that the Boeing 707's instrument panel was as well-illuminated as that of the Volvo 1800. The test was concluded with the comment that the car had left an indelible impression on the tester's mind, as he was sure it would on anyone else lucky enough to drive one.

Just a month later, in May 1966, another Australian road test proclaimed the virtues of the 1800S under the title 'Saucy Swede'. This was Bill Tuckey, writing in *Sports Car World*. He opened his review by telling us that television is a wonderful thing, going on to say that, after a couple of days' driving, he began to feel like 'The Sain't, that television character played by Roger Moore. (That was in the days when British television programmes were exported to Australia, rather than the other way round!) The reviewer continued by telling us that this was probably the most durable, safest and best-made sports car in the world. It seems that already, before the arrival of the 1800, Volvo was a legend in Australia, largely due to the sheer ruggedness of the 122 Amazon, which had proven itself by undertaking anything asked of it by its Antipodean drivers.

It was an interesting observation that the 1800S, apart from naturally possessing all of its elder siblings attributes of toughness, also had an aristocratic, almost feminine, flair that, according to the tester, could only be found in good Swedish furniture or Danish earthenware – a personality of masculine ruggedness and feminine grace. The 1800 was felt to embody both of these qualities. The car tested was the same vehicle as that used by the *Wheels* road test, so it is interesting to compare the results that these two drivers emerged

with. Tuckey was impressed with the small addition to the engine's power output, as it helped to make top gear a little more flexible, though he was somewhat critical of the engine noise at idle and when the throttle was applied with determination, as the SUs audibly sucked for fuel to respond to the demands of the driver.

SPECIFICATIONS

CHASSIS AND BODY DIMENSIONS:

Wheelbase	8 ft 0½ in
Track, front	4 ft 3¾ in
Track, rear	4 ft 3¾ in
Ground clearance	6.5 in
Turning circle	31 ft 6 in
Turns, lock to lock	3¾
Overall length	14 ft 5 in
Overall width	5 ft 7 in
Overall height	4 ft 2½ in

GENERAL INFORMATION:

Steering type	cam and roller
Brake type	disc front, drum rear
Swept area	350 sq in
Suspension, front	coils, wishbones, anti-roll bar
Suspension, rear	coils, trailing radius arms, Panhard rod
Shock absorbers	telescopic
Tyre size	5.90 x 15
Weight (kerb)	2444 lbs
Fuel tank capacity	12 gals
Approx. cruising range	300 miles

ENGINE:

Cylinders	four
Bore and stroke	73.07 mm x 70.01 mm
Cubic capacity	1780 cc
Compression ratio	10 to 1
Fuel requirement	100 octane
Valves	pushrod, overhead
Maximum power	108 bhp at 5800 rpm
Maximum torque	110 lbs/ft at 4000 rpm

TRANSMISSION:

Overall ratios:

First (synchro)	14.25
Second (synchro)	9.08
Third (synchro)	6.20
Fourth (synchro)	4.56
Fourth (overdrive)	3.45
Final drive	4.56 to 1
Mph per 100 rpm in top in OD	21.7 mph

PERFORMANCE

All figures checked to 0.5 percent by Smiths electric tachometer.

Top Speed Average	107.1 mph
Fastest Run	112.5 mph

Maximum, first (6500 rpm limit)	35 mph
Maximum, second (6500 rpm limit)	50 mph
Maximum, third (6500 rpm limit)	79 mph
Maximum, fourth (direct) (6500 rpm limit)	98 mph
Standing quarter mile average	18.4 secs
Fastest run	18.2 secs
0-30 mph	3.7 secs
0-40 mph	6.2 secs
0-50 mph	8.6 secs
0-60 mph	12.4 secs
0-70 mph	19.0 secs
0-80 mph	NA
0-90 mph	NA
0-100 mph	NA
0-110 mph	NA
0-60-0 mph	15.7 secs

	Top	Third
40-60 mph	7.7 secs	6.1 secs
50-70 mph	7.9 secs	7.0 secs
60-80 mph	8.3 secs	6.5 secs
70-90 mph	9.9 secs	— secs
80-100 mph	NA secs	— secs
90-110 mph	NA secs	— secs
100-120 mph	NA secs	— secs
Fuel consumption, cruising	32-34 mpg	
Fuel consumption, overall	27 mpg	

Sports Car World did a road-test data table for the 1800S

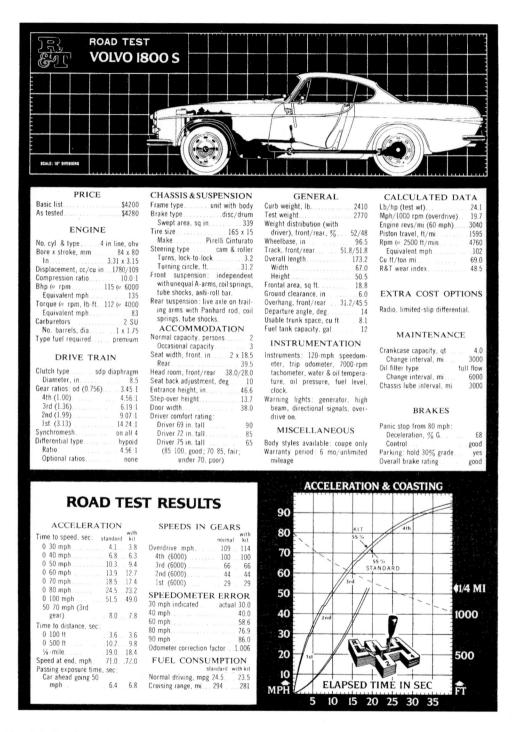

The Road & Track *road test data table for the 1800S.*

The Laycock electric overdrive was highly commended, the operating switch now being on the steering column and very responsive. Just a quick dip of the clutch helped it into place to propel the car to just 100 mph, a bit slower than Barry Cooke's *Wheels* test. The nought-to-sixty time was just a mite slower too, coming in at 13.2 seconds, though Bill Tuckey's standing quarter mile dropped only half a second on his contemporary's time. Throughout this, the ride was said to be outstanding, with shock absorbers and springs working in harmony to take out all the roughness of the sometimes not-so-good roads out of town. A characteristic not often mentioned was the tendency of the 1800S to weave a little when taken on long flat curves in overdrive. Bill Tuckey's solution was to drop into direct top and put down a little throttle to get it back on track. This happens with other cars sometimes, where the power does not seem to be in the right place to hold the car on line at the speed being driven.

The criticisms offered of the car in this review were really, on the admission of its author, quite minor but worthy of mention. He did not like the continuing 'jazzy' instrument panel or the twist-to-lock choke control, but really had fallen in love with all other aspects of the car. Tuckey rounded off his road-test review with the observation that this car stood out as an object lesson to any manufacturer in terms of quality, safety and sensible design, and went on to say that if all Volvos were like the beautifully prepared example he had received for test, then they could put three in the mail for him and his colleagues!

A fascinating road test took place in 1967, in the pages of *The Autocar*, where, in March of that year, a used-car test was conducted on a 1964 Volvo P1800. New, the car had cost just under £1,700 and now it was offered as a used car with 22,200 miles (35,720km) covered for just £1,025, which meant that over one-third of the tax-paid price had eroded in depreciation in the two-and-a half years since the car was sold new. That does not sound too good, until you realize that almost 25 per cent of the new price immediately disappeared in taxes, so the real depreciation, based on the ex-dealer price without taxes, was really quite low. And part of the used price was reflected, it seems, in the fact that there were signs of rust around the wheel rims and bodywork edges. The writer suggested that this was because the car had spent much of its life standing out, but that would not have been all of it. Rim knocks usually occur from kerbing of wheels or clumsy tyre changes, whilst the rusting of bodywork edges most frequently arises from knocks not treated, so it suggests that the car was not especially well cared for by its first owner.

Putting the car through its paces, the tester found that the driver's seat had sagged so that the already-low driving position was now uncomfortable. The engine, on the other hand, seemed to be very close to a new example in responsiveness and there were no problems with the synchromesh in the gearbox; the overdrive was also working well and according to the book. There seemed to be some throttle lag at engine speeds below 3,000rpm, though a tune would almost certainly have cured that, whilst on the road the handling was impeccable except for out-of-balance front wheels. Wear inside the car further suggested that this particular vehicle had not been especially well cared for. Such things as the driver's side armrest covering had split and had not been repaired: the seats showed signs of wear and the engine compartment needed a thorough clean. By and large, the car had endured well the hard life to which it had been subjected and augured well for Volvo's life expectancy.

TOWARDS THE END

With the introduction of the Stromberg-Zenith caburetterod 2-litre engine, a further small increase in power output became available to the 1800 driver. The car remained an '1800' by name, if not by engine size, and *Road Test* magazine in the United States reckoned that while the general improvements to the car were small, they were all worthwhile. For example, the sealed cooling system, the introduction of an alternator in place of the old dynamo to keep the battery up to condition and the multi-way adjustable seats were all commended. The instument panel remained little changed, though, and the steering wheel still resembled something you might find in a Corvette, a Camaro or a Pontiac Grand Prix. One fundamental improvement that was applauded by *Road Test* was the lowering of the engine speed for peak torque, now just 3,500rpm for an increased torque output of 123 lb/ft. This, combined with the reduced exhaust emission, explained why the gross power output of the engine had been increased by so little.

By 1970, *Road & Track* was becoming critical of the 1800, despite it now having a fuel-injected engine (and becoming the 1800E in the process), as well as many interior refinements while also continuing the legend of Volvo durability and reliablity. The fact was that the 1800 was entering its eleventh year and was now competing against cars with all-round independent suspension, plus better performance for the price. As a result, the car was now selling more and more to Volvo enthusiasts and not winning many new customers. On the plus side, for *Road & Track* was noted for throwing brickbats before praise, there was a new gearbox, lifted straight from the 164 saloon, a better power and torque output and the good, honest old-fashioned Volvo predictability in handling. In general performance terms, *Road & Track* put the 1800E into the same league as such unlikely bedfellows as the BMW 2500 and Mercedes-Benz 280SL, whilst its real competitors were now the Alfa Romeo 1750 GTV, the Porsche 914/4, the Lotus Elan coupé and the Triumph GT6.

In performance terms, the 1800E came home with a very respectable 10.1 sec-

OPPOSITE: The Road & Track *road-test data table for the 1800ES.*

LEFT: Inside the 1800E, with leather seats.

ROAD TEST
VOLVO 1800ES

SCALE: 10" DIVISIONS

PRICE

List price, west coast......$5032
Price as tested, west coast...$5340
Price as tested includes standard equipment (overdrive, radial tires, leather upholstery, rear window defroster), AM-FM stereo radio ($212), dealer prep ($95)

IMPORTER

Volvo, Inc.
Rockleigh, N.J. 07647

ENGINE

Type............ohv inline 4
Bore x stroke, mm...89.0 x 80.0
  Equivalent in....3.50 x 3.15
Displacement, cc/cu in...1986/121
Compression ratio.........8.7:1
Bhp @ rpm, net...112 @ 6000
  Equivalent mph......124
Torque @ rpm, lb-ft...115 @ 3500
  Equivalent mph......74
Fuel injection....Bosch electronic
Fuel requirement...regular, 91-oct
Emissions, gram/mile:
  Hydrocarbons..........1.5
  Carbon Monoxide.........28
  Nitrogen Oxides.........2.3

DRIVE TRAIN

Transmission: 4-speed manual
                plus overdrive
Gear ratios: OD (0.797)....3.43:1
  4th (1.00)...........4.30:1
  3rd (1.36)...........5.85:1
  2nd (1.99)...........8.56:1
  1st (3.13)..........13.45:1
Final drive ratio.........4.30:1

CHASSIS & BODY

Layout.....front engine/rear drive
Body/frame...........unit/steel
Brake system: 10.6-in. disc front, 11.6-in. disc rear; vacuum assisted
  Swept area, sq in..........400
Wheels.....styled steel, 15 x 5½ J
Tires...........Goodyear G800
                185/70 HR-15
Steering type........cam & roller
  Overall ratio..........15.5:1
  Turns, lock-to-lock........3.2
  Turning circle, ft........31.5
Front suspension: unequal-length A-arms, coil springs, tube shocks, anti-roll bar

Rear suspension: live axle on upper & lower trailing arms with Panhard rod; coil springs, tube shocks

ACCOMMODATION

Seating capacity, persons...2+2
Seat width, front/rear.2 x 19.0/41.0
Head room, front/rear...35.5/35.5
Seat back adjustment, degrees..40

INSTRUMENTATION

Instruments: 120-mph speedometer, 7000-rpm tach, 99,999 odometer, 999.9 trip odo, oil press, oil temp, coolant temp, fuel level, clock
Warning lights: ammeter, high beam, directionals, hazard flasher, handbrake, overdrive, seatbelt

MAINTENANCE

Service intervals, mi:
  Oil change..............6000
  Filter change...........6000
  Chassis lube............6000
  Minor tuneup............6000
  Major tuneup...........12,000
Warranty, mo/mi.....6/unlimited

GENERAL

Curb weight, lb...........2570
Test weight..............2935
Weight distribution (with driver), front/rear, %....50/50
Wheelbase, in............96.5
Track, front/rear.....51.6/51.6
Length.................172.6
Width..................66.9
Height.................50.4
Ground clearance..........6.1
Overhang, front/rear...30.2/45.9
Usable trunk space, cu ft....10.8
Fuel capacity, U.S. gal.....11.9

CALCULATED DATA

Lb/bhp (test weight).......26.2
Mph/1000 rpm (o'drive)....21.4
Engine revs/mi
  (60 mph o'drive)......2800
Piston travel, ft/mi......1470
R&T steering index......1.02
Brake swept area, sq in/ton...272

RELIABILITY

From R&T Owner Surveys the average number of trouble areas for all models surveyed is 11. As owners of earlier-model Volvos reported 10 trouble areas, we expect the reliability of the Volvo 1800ES to be average.

ROAD TEST RESULTS

ACCELERATION

Time to distance, sec:
  0-100 ft............4.0
  0-500 ft............9.9
  0-1320 ft (¼ mi)....18.2
Speed at end of ¼-mi, mph...74
Time to speed, sec:
  0-30 mph..........3.7
  0-40 mph..........5.6
  0-50 mph..........8.0
  0-60 mph.........11.3
  0-70 mph.........15.5
  0-80 mph.........21.4
  0-90 mph.........30.1

SPEEDS IN GEARS

O'drive (5600 rpm).........116
4th (6500)...............108
3rd (6500)................80
2nd (6500)................56
1st (6500)................36

SPEEDOMETER ERROR

30 mph indicated is actually...28.5
50 mph................47.5
60 mph................57.0
70 mph................66.5
80 mph................75.0
Odometer, 10.0 mi.........9.9

BRAKES

Minimum stopping distances, ft:
  From 60 mph...........178
  From 80 mph...........299
Control in panic stop........good
Pedal effort for 0.5g stop, lb...20
Fade: percent increase in pedal effort to maintain 0.5g deceleration in 6 stops from 60 mph.......50
Parking: hold 30% grade?....yes
Overall brake rating.......good

HANDLING

Speed on 100-ft radius, mph..31.5
Lateral acceleration, g.......0.660

FUEL ECONOMY

Normal driving, mpg........22.5
Cruising range, mi (1-gal res.).245

INTERIOR NOISE

All noise readings in dbA:
  Idle in neutral..........57
  Maximum, 1st gear........84
  Constant 30 mph.........65
    50 mph...............75
    70 mph...............77
    90 mph...............82

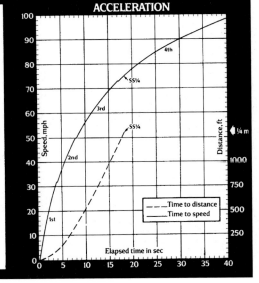

ACCELERATION

onds for nought-to-sixty, whilst the standing quarter mile was a healthy 17.5 seconds and the top speed recorded was 115mph (185km/h). However, there was one fault noted that was really quite surprising of Volvo, or any other car maker for that matter, with blanket speed limits becoming ever more prevalent. That was the level of speedometer error, for at an indicated 30 mph, the true speed was only 26, whilst at an indicated 100, the true speed was 88mph. This represented an error factor of around 12 per cent all the way up the speed range, which was fine if you were looking to stay below the limit, but in the odd cases of minimum speed limits, it was possible to be embarrassed. Ending on a plus, *Road & Track* was delighted to observe that at last, Volvo had ditched the jazzy instrument panel for something a little more sober and a lot more practical. The instruments were now black-faced round dials with clearly readable digits, mounted into a wood-grain fascia, whilst the totally out-of-character two-spoke steering wheel had gone, too.

With Volvo on the brink of ditching the 1800 altogether, the decision to go ahead with Sergio Coggiola's 1800ES seemed uncertain for a while, although it did buy breathing space for the company to consider its future in the sporting car market. As we all now know, the ES was put on the market and it did take the market by surprise, for, returning to *Road & Track*, the question was posed in that publication: 'Who'd have though the Volvo people would turn the 1800 into a sports wagon?' Well, who would have? It was a brave decision, especially as it was not now the first in the field, but it was, according to *Road & Track*, going to be the car to put the sports wagon on the map in the United States, if reactions

were to be judged by those of people first seeing the car.

Coggiola had done a magnificent job with his conversion of the coupé to a sports wagon, for the new model looked complete, not as though something had been stuck on. In fact, if the ES were the first example of the 1800 you had ever seen, you would almost certainly have concluded that it was designed that way from Day One. Small wonder then, that *Road & Track* should conclude that the 1800ES would be 'the one to beat' and destined to be successful despite its dated characteristics and stiff price (it now cost $5,200). However, running right through this road test were signs of mixed feelings about the car. It clearly still had enough performance to rate consideration as a sporting car, and its handling, despite dated chassis characteristics, was still as good as ever. But *Road & Track* could not resist concluding that this was in fact a fine transformation on a car that should have been replaced, not re-vamped. Even so, the tester was firmly of the opinion that Volvo would have no trouble selling the 1800ES.

Car and Driver was very tongue-in-cheek about the whole concept of the sportwagon, making the point that you would never get a piece of eight-by-four plywood into the back without the benefit of a saw, or that overstuffed chair, which would have to be tied to the roof, but then pointed out that the 1800ES was not a station wagon anyway, nor a sports car in the strictest sense of that interpretation. The sportwagon was more of a sporty weekender, a more multi-purpose car than a pure sports car, which by now had outlived much of its usefulness anyway. The young blood could only drive a sports car, but with this machine, he could carry the

VOLVO INTRODUCES A SPORTS CAR THAT REALLY HAULS.

The new Volvo 1800ES is sort of a flying trunk.

It's powered by the same two-litre, computer-controlled, fuel-injected engine as our 1800E sports coupe.

(Car and Driver magazine clocked it from a standstill to 60 in 9.2 seconds.)

But as you see, the 1800ES not only hauls, it carries.

By stretching the roof backward and the trunk floor forward, we've provided a carpeted cargo area 5' x 4' x 22" with the rear seat down. So you can take long vacation gear along when you take a long vacation.

And when you arrive, you won't be in agony. When Car and Driver timed the 1800ES they also sat in it. And declared the leather-upholstered bucket seats "...the most hospitable in the business."

But even more comforting, the 1800ES is a Volvo. And like all Volvos, it's built to last. Which means the 1800ES is a sports car designed to travel slowly on the road to ruin.

A fact you'll appreciate over the long haul.

VOLVO

© 1972, VOLVO, INC. SEE THE DEALER NEAREST YOU AND TEST DRIVE A VOLVO WITH ELECTRONIC FUEL INJECTION. OVERSEAS DELIVERY PLAN AVAILABLE.

Typically powerful advertising from Volvo North America announced the arrival of the 1800ES in the United States, introducing 'a sports car that really hauls!' The 'sportwagon' concept had truly arrived.

149

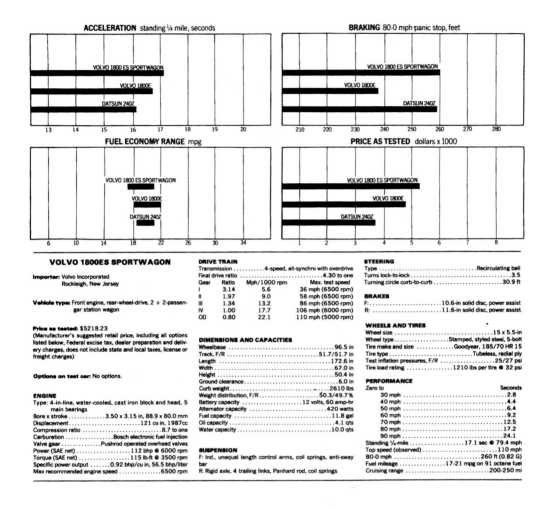

ACCELERATION standing ¼ mile, seconds

VOLVO 1800 ES SPORTWAGON
VOLVO 1800E
DATSUN 240Z

13 14 15 16 17 18 19 20

BRAKING 80-0 mph panic stop, feet

VOLVO 1800 ES SPORTWAGON
VOLVO 1800E
DATSUN 240Z

210 220 230 240 250 260 270 280

FUEL ECONOMY RANGE mpg

VOLVO 1800 ES SPORTWAGON
VOLVO 1800E
DATSUN 240Z

6 10 14 18 22 26 30 34

PRICE AS TESTED dollars x 1000

VOLVO 1800 ES SPORTWAGON
VOLVO 1800E
DATSUN 240Z

1 2 3 4 5 6 7 8

VOLVO 1800ES SPORTWAGON

Importer: Volvo Incorporated
Rockleigh, New Jersey

Vehicle type: Front engine, rear-wheel-drive, 2 + 2-passenger station wagon

Price as tested: $5218.23
(Manufacturer's suggested retail price, including all options listed below, Federal excise tax, dealer preparation and delivery charges, does not include state and local taxes, license or freight charges)

Options on test car: No options.

ENGINE
Type: 4-in-line, water-cooled, cast iron block and head, 5 main bearings
Bore x stroke ....3.50 x 3.15 in, 88.9 x 80.0 mm
Displacement.......................121 cu in, 1987cc
Compression ratio ....8.7 to one
Carburation ....Bosch electronic fuel injection
Valve gear ....Pushrod operated overhead valves
Power (SAE net) ....112 bhp @ 6000 rpm
Torque (SAE net) ....115 lb-ft @ 3500 rpm
Specific power output ....0.92 bhp/cu in, 56.5 bhp/liter
Max recommended engine speed ....6500 rpm

DRIVE TRAIN
Transmission ....4-speed, all-synchro with overdrive
Final drive ratio ....4.30 to one

Gear	Ratio	Mph/1000 rpm	Max. test speed
I	3.14	5.6	36 mph (6500 rpm)
II	1.97	9.0	58 mph (6500 rpm)
III	1.34	13.2	86 mph (6500 rpm)
IV	1.00	17.7	106 mph (6000 rpm)
OD	0.80	22.1	110 mph (5000 rpm)

DIMENSIONS AND CAPACITIES
Wheelbase ....96.5 in
Track, F/R ....51.7/51.7 in
Length ....172.6 in
Width ....67.0 in
Height ....50.4 in
Ground clearance................................6.0 in
Curb weight.............................≈ 2610 lbs
Weight distribution, F/R.....................50.3/49.7 %
Battery capacity ....12 volts, 60 amp-hr
Alternator capacity ....420 watts
Fuel capacity ....11.8 gal
Oil capacity ....4.1 qts
Water capacity ....10.0 qts

SUSPENSION
F: Ind., unequal length control arms, coil springs, anti-sway bar
R: Rigid axle, 4 trailing links, Panhard rod, coil springs

STEERING
Type ....Recirculating ball
Turns lock-to-lock 3.5
Turning circle curb-to-curb ....30.9 ft

BRAKES
F:........................10.6-in solid disc, power assist
R: ....11.6-in solid disc, power assist

WHEELS AND TIRES
Wheel size ....15 x 5.5-in
Wheel type...................Stamped, styled steel, 5-bolt
Tire make and size ....Goodyear, 185/70 HR 15
Tire type ....Tubeless, radial ply
Test inflation pressures, F/R ....25/27 psi
Tire load rating ....1210 lbs per tire @ 32 psi

PERFORMANCE

Zero to	Seconds
30 mph	2.8
40 mph	4.4
50 mph	6.4
60 mph	9.2
70 mph	12.5
80 mph	17.2
90 mph	24.1

Standing ¼-mile ....17.1 sec @ 79.4 mph
Top speed (observed) ....110 mph
80-0 mph ....260 ft (0.82 G)
Fuel mileage ....17-21 mpg on 91 octane fuel
Cruising range ....200-250 mi

The Car and Driver *1800ES road-test data table.*

equipment of a long weekend and still have a car worthy of showing off in – it's called 'posing' today. The real magic of this last-of-the-line 1800 was the fact that it really was useful and capable of a sub-ten-second nought-to-sixty at the same time. The standing quarter was now 17.1 seconds and top speed an honest 110 mph (177km/h). Given that you would be hard pressed to get your golf clubs or aqualung into an MGB GT, this was the ultimate way to carry your weekend gear, and partner, in speed and style.

10 Success Begets Success – From 1800 to C70 Coupé

It is fairly pretty clear that the Volvo 1800ES confirmed a trend in the world's car markets. It could, had Carrozzeria Coggiola been brought on to the scene a little earlier and the fruits of Sergio Coggiola's work been put into production as soon as it was complete, have even set that trend. For it was in the minds of Volvo designers to produce a sports wagon long before it came to David Ogle and Reliant. But Volvo did not move that quickly, not least because it wanted whatever it did to be right when it went into the market place. In any event, the whole 1800 exercise had been a costly one for Volvo in the early days and it did not want to get its fingers burnt again. Certainly, there had been some relief from the early body problem when the car switched to being produced in Sweden and, co-incidentally, when Rootes had taken over the Linwood factory, together with the body pressings contract.

It became apparent to Volvo that, after killing off the 1800ES in 1973, there was a market niche worth retaining in just that sector of the sporty car market – the sports wagon, as *Road & Track* had so skilfully dubbed it. But a replacement was to be a long time coming, as Volvo had a few other things to do first, not least the development of the Volvo Concept Car and the Light Component Project (LCP) programme, partly funded by the Swedish government.

But Volvo did not abandon sporty cars altogether, producing the 262 coupé in the mid- to late-1970s, though this was not the same kind of sports car as the 1800 had been, being simply an adaptation of a saloon model.

The LCP programme was the one that was to be of interest in the development of the next sporting Volvo, as it was to be used to develop, apart from the use of lightweight composites in the body structure, front-wheel drive. Volvo had never yet built a front-wheel drive until this programme was begun, with ex-Saab designer Rolfe Mellde very much in the thick of it. Many people had expected the 1800ES to be quite quickly replaced by a front-wheel drive model as a consequence of Mellde joining Volvo, but that was not the plan at Gothenburg. Front-wheel drive was certainly part of the programme, but the successor to the 1800 was a long way off yet. And when it did come, it was not built in Sweden. History repeating itself? No, not quite.

THE SPORTS CAR THAT MIGHT HAVE BEEN

Not long before Volvo brought about the demise of the Jensen contract, Jan Wilsgaard took a trip to the United States. He was already convinced that he should be

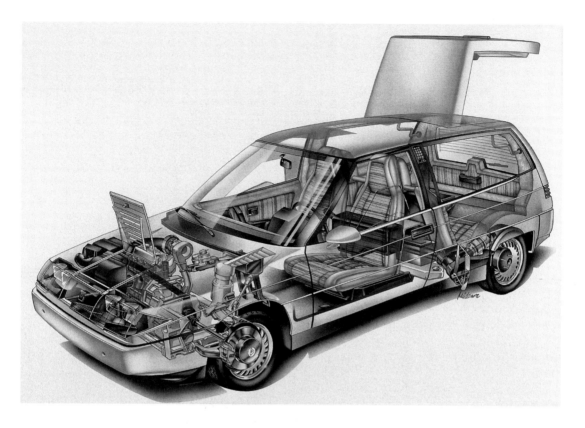

Volvo's LCP experimental car continued, in theory at least, the sportwagon concept, but also was aimed at establishing the concept of unitized assembly and exchange.

considering a replacement for the 1800 and had taken more than a passing look at the Ford Mustang, bearing in mind that the United States would be the biggest market for whatever the car became. The immediate success of the Mustang convinced Wilsgaard that this was a good market slot to aim for. It had already been said that the 1800 was a bit cramped and so the Volvo board was becoming convinced that there was a case for a larger sporting model. Wilsgaard took the opportunity to examine the market.

A substantial portfolio of drawings and two-dimensional sketches was prepared on Wilsgaard's return to Gothenburg and a selection placed before the board to choose

examples to go to prototype stage. Two were selected and the process of making models approved. P16S was the designation given to the project, and the idea was to build a car based on the mechanical components of the six-cylinder-engined 164 Saloon, although using a wheelbase that was 10cm shorter than the 164. The engine and gearbox would come from the 164, the 2,978cc power unit generating 180bhp SAE at 6,000rpm. It was originally thought that three SU carburettors would be fitted, but tuning was foreseen as a problem, so a switch to fuel injection was made in the interests of maintaining a state of tune and providing a cleaner running engine.

As the project progressed, its number was changed to P172 and scale models went into build. The final design selection was for a car of more angular lines than the P1800, perhaps more like a hybrid of something which would yet emerge from the house of Pininfarina, combined with the best from Pontiac a decade and a half later. Distinctly a two-plus-two, with real space for the rear seat passengers, the P172 did not really look like a grand touring coupé, but more like a short-bodied, two-door American sedan. But then, the Pontiac GTO did not look much like a grand touring coupé either. So, the design specification progressed, as the potential successor to the P1800 progressed. By now, the 1800 had ceased to be assembled in West Bromwich and so a need was felt to proceed to something from which a positive decision could be made.

It was now time to approve the construction of a full-size clay model and advance the performance requirements of the P172, so that, among other things, a costing exercise could be embarked upon to verify the feasibility of the project as a production model. In order for the car to make its mark, it had to turn in 125mph (200km/h), with an eight-second nought-to-sixty time. In order to achieve this, a low body weight was called for and the prospect of constructing the car with alloy panels was considered, but the cost was prohibitive and so steel panelling was to be the way ahead, just as in the 1800. Now, a full-scale model was approved to determine the final line, and it seemed likely that the new model would find its way into production.

By September 1966, the full-size clay model was available for its first showing. It was painted dark blue and placed out-

The P172 Sports coupé development prototype was an experiment aimed at creating a larger sporting model for the Volvo market, but like many more 'concept' cars, went nowhere.

Based on the 3-litre six-cylinder-engined 164, this Volvo 3000GTZ was built as a styling exercise by Zagato.

side to give a more realistic atmosphere in which to view it. The board went for it and laid down plans for serious production at Olofstrom. Initial market research suggested that the car would sell in the United States at a price tag of $6,000, and on that basis, plans were laid for a first production run of 10,000 cars (the same number as had been set for the initial production run of P1800s between Scotland and West Bromwich). The target for the first series was 50,000 cars and production was to start in August 1969. In the end, however, the board of directors got cold feet and during the spring of 1967, Project P172 was cancelled, despite all the development work and costs incurred so far. We will never know how the car might have sold, but in the light of the developments that took place across the rest of the world's automotive industry, there's every reason to suppose that it would, in fact, have been a success. But it was not to be and the actual successor to the P1800 was now some years away and would take a very different form.

VOLVO'S FIRST FRONT WHEEL DRIVE CAR

If one does not count the LCP, which was purely a development vehicle, then Volvo's first front-wheel drive vehicle was in fact the successor to the 1800ES. It was the 480ES, originally code-named E12. It seemed pretty obvious to most observers that Volvo would take this step once it had agreed a collaborative deal with Renault, and later Peugeot, in France to develop engines and transmissions for future cars. This had much to do with the need to reduce production costs of components in the wake of a very difficult period for the whole of Europe's automotive industry in the 1970s. Volvo had also tied a deal with DAF in 1972, which had formed the basis of Volvo Car BV, Volvo Car Corporation's Dutch subsidiary. Problems had arisen in a number of areas, all at the same time. Firstly, the Volvo 343, a development of the small DAF, did not win the market response hoped for and then, in its wake, the 200 series of cars was running into cor-

Pehr Gustaf Gyllenhammar

You might not expect that family connections would have much to do with the appointment of only the third chief executive of one of the fastest growing industrial corporations on the continent of Europe. But that's exactly how it was. Pehr Gyllenhammar was not only Gustaf Engellau's son-in-law, he was only thirty-six years old when he was appointed in 1971.

Gyllenhammar's perspective of Volvo was not just car-orientated. He took a total view of Volvo's industrial activities on a global scale. He endorsed the production of the 1800ES sporting station wagon, but it was also his decision to endorse the production of an all-terrain vehicle, the C300, that brought the 1800ES's production to an abrupt halt. Profitability from space was the deciding factor, so the 1800 had to go. In only his second year of office, Volvo took over the Dutch DAF car company and it was from the Dutch factory that the 1800ES's successor, the 480, emerged with Pehr Gyllenhammar's approval.

New factories were built in Sweden and the close link with Renault was forged largely by Gyllenhammar. It was was he who set up the co-operative engine deal between Volvo, Renault and Peugeot, and it was the V-6 engine that resulted from that co-production agreement which went into the ill-fated De Lorean sports car produced in Belfast. That engine deal was only the precursor, though, to something much bigger.

The man who brought about the Volvo-Renault alliance was Pehr Gustaf Gyllenhammar.

In September 1993, an agreement was concluded for the merger of Volvo with Renault. Few people in the European motor industry could really see it working, for the two corporate entities did not have common backgrounds or goals, other than survival and profit. Many members of Volvo's senior management and board opposed the deal and in a board meeting on 2 December 1993, Pehr Gyllenhammar resigned from the board. But he had achieved a great deal for his company, firstly having increased the number of employees by over 30 per cent and the corporate turnover from an already amazing 6,000 million kronor to a staggering 100,000 million – a growth of seventeen-fold.

rosion problems, something previously unheard of in Volvo cars, which had built their entire reputation on durability.

Pehr Gustaf Gyllenhammar was Chief Executive of Volvo at the time and it was he who had sealed the deal with Renault and Peugeot. The prime thrust of the agreement between the three was the need for a new V-6 engine to power the largest of their cars,

Volvo's 260 (and later the 760), Renault's 35 and Peugeot's 505 (later 605) models. Behind that prime objective, though, was the additional benefit of co-operative production of smaller engines, in particular the power unit for the 480 and for the new Volvo front-wheel drive small saloon, the 440, which was aimed at replacing the 360 model. Both would be built in Holland.

The 480ES shows a direct connection with the LCP, in style and concept, though its connection with the 1800ES is also clear. This car sported a 1.7-litre Renault engine.

The design exercise for the 480ES began in 1978, with two objectives in mind. The first was to fill the gap, particularly in the United States, left behind by the demise of the 1800ES, though much of that gap was already being filled by products from the Orient. But the second, and perhaps more important, objective was to produce a 'flagship' for the new small Volvo family car, the 440. Styling exercises were considered both from Holland and from Gothenburg, where the ultimate control lay for the decision. A design clinic was held in 1981 in the United States, where a carefully selected band of potential customers saw the design models of the cars under consideration and compared them with existing car types, feeding back preferences and feelings about the designs before them. The design ultimately chosen for production was the Dutch one and so, under the direction of an Englishman, Geoffrey Wright,

who had migrated from his post as Technical Director of Chrysler United Kingdom, the project was advanced to the prototype stage.

Recalling the experience of the 1800ES's development, and because of Volvo's cautious approach to everything, The company was beaten to a market launch by another car that bore a striking resemblance in certain detail to the new model. This time it was Honda who beat Volvo to the draw, with the Accord Aerodeck, launched in the spring of 1985, a whole year ahead of the Volvo 480ES. Once again, there was nothing Volvo could do: it had already invested a huge sum of money in the development of the 480 and so felt forced to forge ahead. This experience forced Volvo to restructure its design and development activities so as to shorten lead times between concept and production.

Inside the Volvo 480ES. It was quite a roomy car for its size, though a 'sporty' coupé/wagon rather than a 'sports' coupé.

The dashboard of the 480ES was clear to see and everything was easy to reach.

The Volvo/Renault 1.7 engine/transmission.

OLD CONCEPTS NEW DESIGN – PRESERVING THE TRADITION

The body design of the 480ES deliberately showed positive links to its predecessor. It was a two-plus-two sport wagon, though 12.5cm shorter and 1cm wider. Gone were the chrome-trimmed fins, to be replaced

with a moulded line through to the rear end of the car. The essentially heavy bumpers were carefully and tastefully blended into the front and rear ends of the car, avoiding that awful grafted-on appearance of bumpers on so many cars of the period. The tail-light cluster was neatly blended into the rear quarter panel below the almost all-glass tailgate – another link

This rear quarter view shows a well-balanced clean line.

with the past – whilst the headlights were of the 'pop-up' type, with driving lamps positioned to the outside of them. Built into the tailgate was a wash–wipe arm that was activated automatically when the driver selected reverse gear whilst the front windscreen wipers were operating.

Inside the 480ES, the instrumentation was typically comprehensive, with the usual large speedometer and tachometer dials. But a computer provided the rest of the information, including fuel and oil levels; inside and outside air temperatures; fuel consumption and anticipated remaining range; oil and coolant temperatures. The computer also controlled the interior lighting, the central locking and burglar alarm, as well as, believe it or not, the automatic headlights. That's right, automatic headlights, which switched themselves off 30 seconds after locking the car at night, so as to allow the occupant to see his or her way into the house after parking up. Fine,

if you drive your car nose-first on to your drive and not into the garage. And what was the advantage if you reversed your car on to the drive or into the garage, as every responsible driver should?

The engine was the result of the Volvo–Renault development of a 1,721cc overhead camshaft transversely located unit for front-wheel drive. Volvo was the first of the two companies to use the new engine, in the 480ES. Porsche Design gave extensive help in the development of the fuel-injection system. Oddly, this new engine was labelled B18, though it was a new unit, with belt-driven single overhead camshaft, and it produced 109bhp at 5,800rpm. Transmission was a five-speed synchromesh unit as standard and the car's top speed was reckoned to be 118mph (190km/h), a pretty respectable performance, whilst nought-to-sixty time was 9.4 seconds. A later development of the B18 engine was the B18FT, a power unit

Inside, the luggage compartment was not large with the two back seats up, but when they were folded, it gave quite a lot of space and it was very accessible.

equipped with a catalytic converter for clean running and a turbocharger for improved performance. This engine came up with 120bhp and had a water-cooled turbo.

The key advantage of the turbocharger was not the improvement of top speed or acceleration, though acceleration was naturally improved: it was mainly aimed at improving the low-speed torque output. Peak torque in the turbo unit was produced at 1,800rpm, whereas in the naturally aspirated engine, the engine speed was much higher. In fact, Volvo, with assistance from Porsche, managed to produce an almost straight-line torque curve between 1,800rpm and 4,600rpm, which made a substantial difference to everyday han-

dling of the car. This was achieved by the installation of an electronic boost control. It was a very advanced engine control concept and the engine was notably clean running, though it has been said in more recent years that reliability of running suffered from the 'gadgetry'. Whether that's down to a matter of design or maintenance is perhaps a moot point.

Suspension in the 480 was somewhat different from the 1800. At the front there was a Macpherson strut, with widely spaced wishbones and an anti-roll bar, whilst at the back there was a dead axle with Watts linkage and a Panhard rod to hold it all together. The engine, gearbox and lower wishbones of the suspension unit were assembled together on to a subframe which was mounted in rubber bushings. As a consequence of this set-up, the handling characteristics of the new car were said to be outstanding. You could throw it around far more exuberantly than its predecessor and it was reasonably economical. But it was not to find its way into its original target market and it was to be plagued with reliability problems that were the result of electronics failures.

PROBLEMS WITH THE PRICE AND THE PRODUCT

Some months after the 480ES's announcement in 1986, the car was launched into several European markets and found its way into more during 1987. But the Wall Street panic which resulted in 'Black Monday', 18 October 1987, caused the dollar to fall against the guilder by 32 per cent, which meant a hike in the intended showroom price of the 480 to over $20,000, whereas the plan had been to sell it at around $15,000. Rather than be slated for a grossly overpriced car, and taking into account US dealer reactions to the problems over the 360 and the 200 series, Volvo decided to cut its losses and just not offer the 480 into the US market at all, so the 1800ES never did get a replacement, except that the field was now left clear for Honda and the Aerodeck.

In fact, it is probably as well that the 480 did not reach US shores in line with the original plan, because shortly after its introduction – just over 2,000 cars had

The tail-light cluster was neat, clean and simple, though not cheap to replace.

Latest in the line is the Volvo C70 Coupé.

been delivered – serious complaints began to flood in about problems with starting the engine, with headlights not working and with instrument readings being either non-existent or wildly inaccurate. Volvo did not need this kind of problem, especially after the painful experience of the 360 and the rust problems with the 200 series. Volvo had an enviable reputation for quality and durability, which it was determined to protect as best it could. So it decided, at an ultimate cost of around ten million kronor, to recall all those early cars and hit the prroblem head on. The root cause was found to be the control computer and once this was sorted out, the car went back on sale and upheld the corporation's reputation of quality and reliability. Sadly, though, less than 20,000 cars reached their

various markets by the end of 1987. Even so, the 480 continued to sell right up to its demise in 1995, not quite reaching the eleven-year mark, but making room for the newest of Volvo's sporty coupés.

LATEST OF THE LINE – THE C70

In 1997, Volvo introduced a double, within hours of each other at two different shows – one in London, the other in Detroit. Looking back to the days of 'The Saint' and his West Bromwich-built Volvo P1800, the company, having designed and built its latest coupé, managed to get the newest car into a film of Leslie Charteris' famous character. So Simon Templar

The C70 general interior and dashboard, showing a deceptively roomy cabin.

rides again, and in a Volvo once more. But this newest of Gothenburg coupés was no longer cramped or eccentric. It is the epitome of design elegance, built with all of Volvo's traditions and established concepts, but bringing a few new ones with it. Styled in-house by a team led by British design chief Peter Horbury, this car was deliberately pitched at the upper end of the coupé market, competing head on with Alfa Romeo's GTV, Lancia's Kappa, the Mercedes Benz CLK and SL coupés, Mitsubishi's 3000 and Rover's 800 coupé. Some were more expensive, some were a lot less expensive, but Volvo decided to trade blatantly on the aspiration value of its product – that many people running less expensive cars aspired to own the Volvo.

As with all Volvo sporting models, the C70 was based on the floorpan of a saloon model, this time the 850, though with a shorter wheelbase. It used the five-cylinder, twenty-valve engine from the 850 (which also found its way into the V70, the saloon and station wagon successors to the 850), in naturally aspirated and turbocharged forms. The naturally aspirated engine produced 193bhp, whilst the turbo version put out 240bhp and in this form, using the five-speed manual gearbox (a four-speed automatic was also available), the car was capable of reaching 60mph from a standstill in just 6.9 seconds – rather exciting for car that would carry four up in complete comfort.

Inside, the C70 was unashamed luxury, with leather, fine fabrics and wood everywhere, even on the steering wheel (a Volvo

Even from the rear, the C70 is a very elegant car.

with a wood-rim steering wheel, that's right!) The T5, turbocharged, model possessed superb handling and was available with lowered suspension to make it an even more exciting drive. Top speed was 150 mph (240km/h), although this car could be driven at high speed without realizing it, for interior noise was minimal and the 17 or 18in cast spoke alloy wheels with either 225/45ZR17 Michelin or 225/40ZR18 Pirelli wide-aspect ratio tyres held the car down like a limpet. The suspension, of course, had a contribution to make, too. Volvo's new Deltalink rear suspension system allowed the rear wheels to turn fractionally into the steering arc on a bend. This, in conjunction with the independent front suspension, kept the tyres in maximum contact with the ground and minimized body roll in the turn.

Inside the C70 was one of the safest places you could be on the road. Furthermore, the list of standard interior equipment and fittings was like reading the whole accessories catalogue for many another make of car. It included: driver and passenger temperature controls; air conditioning; a pollen filter, electric front windows; tinted glass all round; automatic front seat-belt height adjustment; CD stereo radio cassette unit with (believe it or not) ten speakers to provide Dolby 'surround sound', electrically adjustable front seats with memory, internal luggage compartment and fuel flap release. As if that was not a long enough list, the car also had side impact bars and airbags, driver's airbag, anti-lock brakes with electronic brake distribution, headlamp adjustment, headlamp wash–wipe, front seat-belt pre-tensioners, a deadlocking system which featured anti-theft alarm and immobiliser and remote central locking. What a list – but then, what a car!

The 'double' part of this stage of the story involves the first drophead Volvo since the Glasspar-bodied P1900 of the 1950s and the first volume produced soft-top since before World War II. Peter Horbury explained in an interview that if you looked at any previous Volvo since the 140, the body waistline always rose from the front the rear. But on the C70, that line arched from front to rear. Effectively, the waistline had been inverted in the cause of creating a drophead, which had been designed alongside the coupé. The new C70 convertible incorporated all the safety and mechanical features of the coupé, as well as having substantially reinforced wind-screen pillars to contribute to the rollover protection for the occupants. The other part of the rollover protection involved two pop-up protective bars behind the rear seats, so

preventing the car from rolling on to the passengers. The power hood retracted beneath a lift-up rear tonneau panel so that, with the top down, the car looked as clean as any coupé.

The whole idea of producing both coupé and convertible examples of the C70 was really quite an old one in the motor industry – certainly in the British industry, anyway. The concept of producing a sports car to attract motorists into 'the clan' of one make usually achieves a long-term retention of that customer, loyal to the make. MG, in particular, used this technique, selling an inexpensive sports car to young men who would eventually marry and buy an MG family car in later years. In Volvo's case, the same principle applied, though moved up-market. Here, the well-to-do young driver, male or female, would buy the C70 and graduate from it to a family Volvo – a V70 saloon or station wagon. As this book takes to the press, the Volvo C70 coupé and con-vertible are the most advanced and exciting sporting Volvos yet offered.

11 Buying, Owning and Enjoying an 1800

Among all the classic sports cars available in the world, why on earth would you want to own a Volvo 1800? After all, you could go for an MGA, a Triumph TR3, TR3A or TR4, an Alfa Romeo Giulietta or Giulia, a Porsche 356, a Sunbeam Alpine or an MGB. If it's a purpose built coupé you want, then the Triumphs drop off the list and whilst the Sunbeam is not a coupé by design, its hardtop was a very snug fit and since the doors had wind-up windows, it was effectively a coupé. But then you could ask why anyone might want an MGA or an Alfa Romeo, because they were 'rotboxes'. Truth is, they all were, because the process of metal preservation treatment was very poorly done and developments in that area over the last twenty years have been enormous. It will be interesting to see, though, how restorable the enthusiast finds the 'protected metal' cars of today in thirty years' time.

SELECTING YOUR CAR

By and large, there are two things that attract a would-be enthusiast to the Volvo 1800. The first is the reputation Volvo has had over many years for the safety and durability of its cars. The second is the fact that this car is, in many ways, 'different'. Its styling was distinctive and its engine was virtually unburstable. So the first thing any would-be owner of an 1800 has to do is examine the market and select his or her car. The most important thing to note here is that Volvo 1800s are pretty rare, because there weren not many made in the first place and whilst the majority went to the United States, there are probably less survivors per 100,000 cars of the population in the US than in Great Britain. That said, the worst thing you can possibly do is to buy the first one you see on the basis that it might be a long time before you see another. Buy it if it is sound, but if it is falling to pieces, let it go until you find another. And you will find another if you're patient – they are about, and they do come on to the market.

As is true of so many enthusiast cars, the best way to find a car if you do not have one of your choice now is to join a club associated with that make and, if one exists, the model of the car of your choice. There is a Volvo Owners' Club in Great Britain and a Volvo Enthusiasts' Club for the older classics. You can join a club without owning a car and often, but probably not enough, potential owners follow that route to obtaining the model of their choice. Unless you are a competent motor engineer or mechanic, it is unwise to buy a car entirely alone, without any kind of support from someone with relevant expertise. This is more relevant to bodywork, perhaps, than mechanical components, because it is often true that the mechanical components are more readily renovatable than the body – a point almost certainly true of the Volvo 1800.

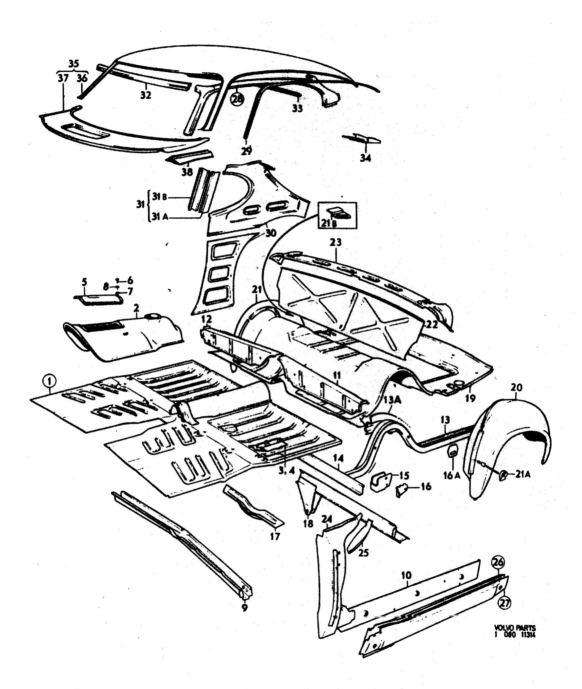

This exploded view of the centre section of the body pressing set for the 1800 coupé shows the areas particularly vulnerable to rust and the original shapes of each element of the assembly. The sills and rear wheel arches were especially vulnerable.

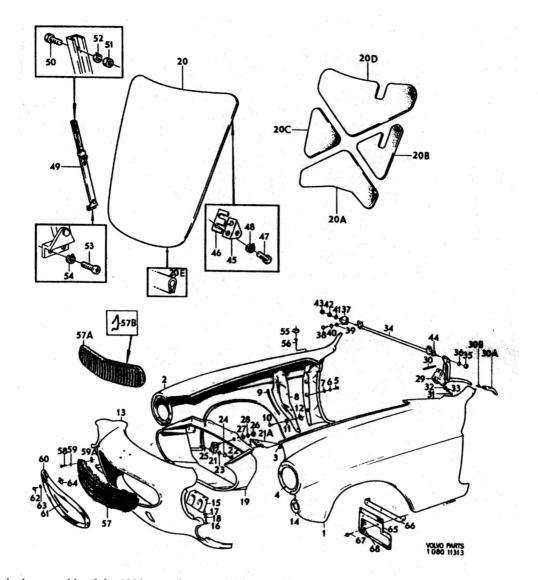

The body assembly of the 1800 was always a fairly complicated set of pressings, as you begin to realize when you look at this set for the front body outer panels...

Taking up the issue of body condition, when viewing your potential dream car, you must recognize that, despite the Volvo car's reputation for longevity, this model seems not to be typical. There are all kinds of little moisture traps in the 1800 bodyshell, as a consequence of which even a car that has been garaged for most of its life can become a 'rotbox'. Part of the problem is that many of the metal protection processes used in the 1950s and 1960s did anything but protect metal. For example,

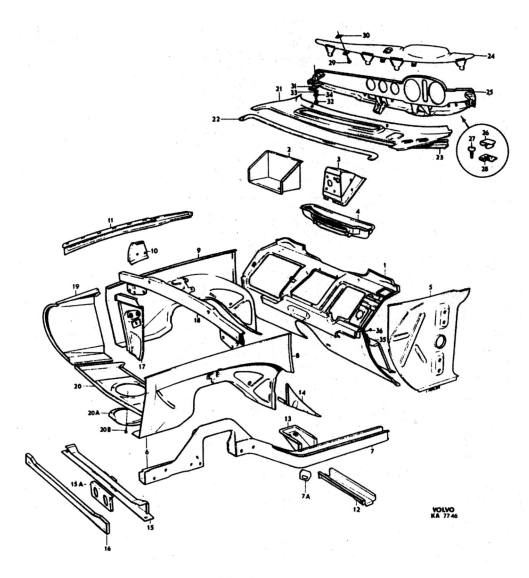

...followed by the inner body set. Rust could gather in several places here.

many underbody sealants used in those days put a quite thick coating of protective material on the underside of the body which, in time, became hard and cracked or chipped. Once this had happened, there was an opportunity for water to enter,

which inevitably it did, and the underbody sealant did its job in reverse, by holding in the moisture which, in company with the inflow of air as the car moved along the road, did its worst and ultimately caused oxidation – rust.

Vent or drain holes were – and still are – the next problem in body designs, because too often they clog and owners do nothing about it, often because they do not even realize the holes are there. And finally, there are the little water traps that the designers either overlooked or did not think were especially significant at the time that the cars went into production. The Volvo 1800 seems to be endowed with all of the features described and so rust can be a problem over a large area of the bodywork, especially the sills (or rocker panels) beneath the doors and around the rear wheel arches.

DOING THE BODY CHECK

Starting with the sills, when looking at a car to buy, check both the outers and the inners for structural integrity. It may sound silly, but if you have a magnet you can put in your pocket when you go to examine a car, it would be a good idea to take it with you. Why? Because you can't see what's metal and what's filler beneath a half-convincing paint job and many of these cars have had paintwork replaced (renewed, touched-in or bodged?) since they left whichever factory they were assembled in. If the outer sill seems to respond favourably to the magnet test (that the magnet grabs at the metal and hangs on), then try knocking along the sill with your knuckles to see if it's solid. If it is, then the chances are that the inner sill might be okay, too – 'Might be', because the outer could, of course, have been replaced and the inner one not. So lift the carpet adjacent to the sill and check the inner in the same way. If it capsizes or threatens to – if it's obviously weak because you can see rust in any quantity – then look no further

and leave it alone. All you have to do is be patient and another one will come along.

Your alternative is to face the fact that to replace the sills, the front wing (fender) will have to be removed and a chunk of the bottom of the rear one, too, which presents quite a major cosmetic exercise. The problem with the sills is that there is a drain hole and drain holes rarely find themselves being cleaned out, so they block and, guess what, they rust. On the 1800, there is a channel which guides water down the front edges of the doors and culminates in a drain hole between the front wing and the sill. Owners of new cars rarely even think about such things so, in the first year or so of the car's life, it has a perfect opportunity to collect water. And because our rainwater is anything but pure, it does not take long to erode the paint in vital areas, then 'metal mouse' attacks and leaves the unsuspecting next owner with a developing problem which, by the time the car reaches its third owner, is a time bomb, ticking away to challenge the observation skills of an enthusiast just like you.

The rear wheel arches also rust badly where the inner and outer panels come together, as water tends to collect in the channel around the boot (trunk) lid aperture. This brings a further problem, for not only do the wheel arches become weak, but that same water is then allowed into the floorpan below the rear seats, so you will need to remove them, too, just to check. Again, the same message: if there's serious rust, leave the car alone and wait for another one to come along, because the whole floorpan is vulnerable. You need to check that, anyway, especially around the area of the jacking points. It would not be difficult to imagine an 1800 with a rear end floorpan that actually lets in light where it meets the wheel arches and boot structure. And you know what that will mean to your bank balance if you buy a car in that state!

Inside the front wings (fenders) is a splash panel, which by the very nature of its function, is prone to rust. If it has rusted to the point of penetration, then expect to find a line of rust down the front wing just behind the position of that splash panel. If you can see it on the outside, then it has come through from the inside. The inner wings, too, the box sections that run along above the front wheels inside the 'pretty bit', often fail, but these can, with a bit of manipulation, be replaced with Volvo 120 types (if you can still find them), because they are of a very similar shape. The other problem with the front wings is the headlight mountings, under the chrome surrounds. Water collects here and often near-terminal damage has been done. Front wings are not easy things to fit, as the windscreen has to come to do the job properly – and there's another problem in the making.

If somebody has removed the windscreen for any reason, and the most com-

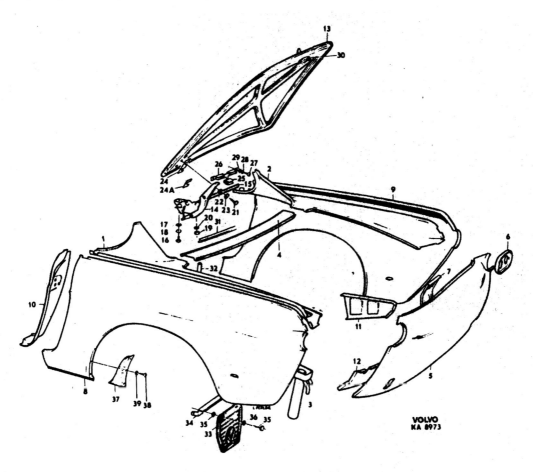

Here's the coupé rear body assembly outer panels, the inners being part of the centre section assembly.

mon is because of breakage, then if the seal has not been properly relocated, or replaced, water can get inside the outer lip of the seal. If it does not get right through and drip into your lap, you may never know about it until it's too late, when the bottom of the windscreen pillar has rotted away, or even the windscreen mounting lip has suffered such damage as to make it difficult to

repair the bodywork. This is not a common problem with 1800s, but it might just be worth a check to see if the screen has been replaced, because that should lead you into a bit of further investigation, just for safety.

Drain holes, again, are a cause of other problems. The boot floor's survival is dependent upon whether or not the drain

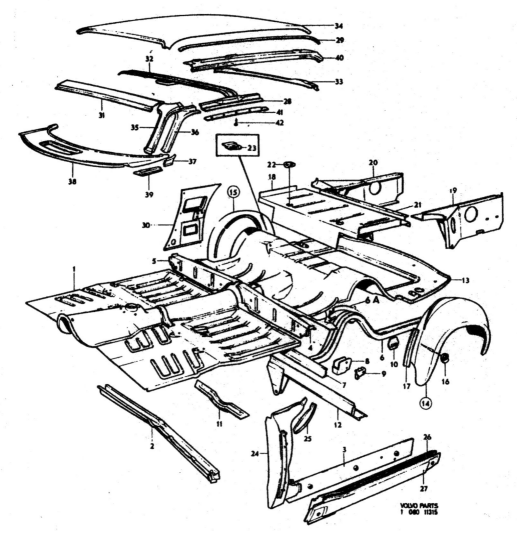

The key difference between the panel set for the coupé and that for the ES was the roof panel which, on the ES, was longer and flatter.

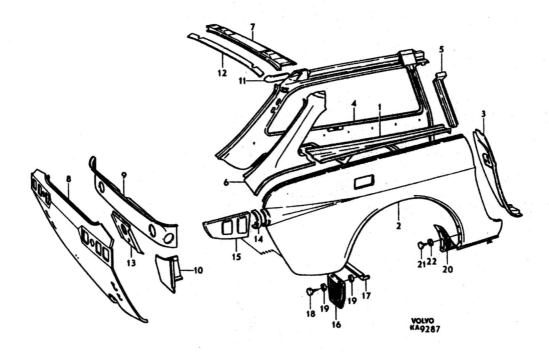

The rear end of the ES panel set was essentially the coupé panels with the add-ons of the extended upper panels, mating up to the rear wings in place of the luggage compartment.

tubes are clear, or even there! The fact is that they can be knocked off and then all the water that would be bypassing the boot in normal circumstances finishes up on the floor and will wash around there until it makes its own escape. The fuel filler flap also suffers from a blocked drain hole and so it rots around the hinge and, you've guessed it, falls off. Lastly, look at the front and rear valances when you go underneath the car (you will go underneath it to have a look, won't you?), as they tend to suffer the ravages of time. This is because it was often not convenient, in the car's early life, for the owner to give much attention to the areas below the bumpers (and who cleans the collected muck of years from the inner edges of the front and rear valances, anyway?). Therefore the valances were rarely

cleaned: and if they were cleaned, they were rarely polished, and if they were even on occasion polished, they were rarely, if ever, cleaned off on their inside ledges to remove gathered mud. Result? Rotten valances. Out of all this, you will have realized that you need to check your prospective purchase over very carefully and if it has most or all of the faults detailed here, then sit on your cash.

THE 1800's ENGINE AND GEARBOX

By and large, the B18 and B20 engines have always been known for durability and their capacity to withstand abuse. You can come across a car with over 150,000

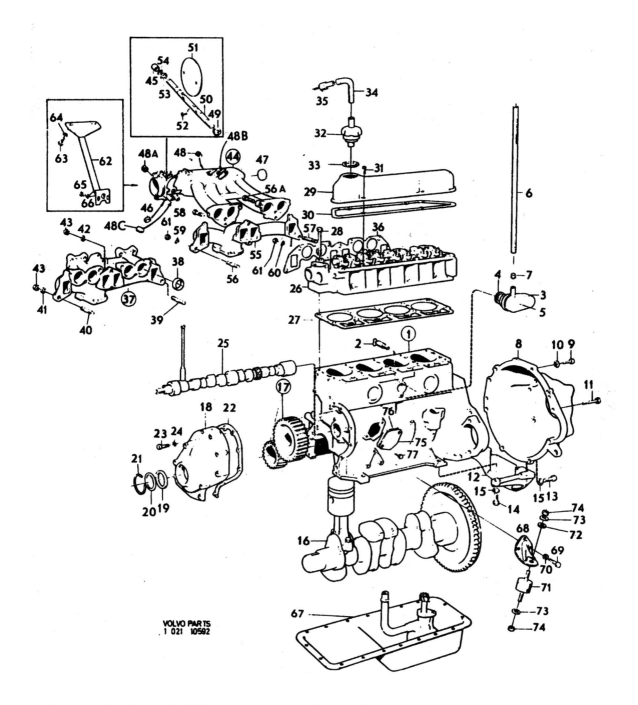

This exploded view of the 1800 engine gives an indication of the robustness of the unit and of the differences between carburettor-fuelled and injection-fuelled installations.

recorded miles that goes as though it's just been run in. The fact is, if it was run in carefully and the car has been well looked after generally, you could probably put at least another 50,000 on it without doing anything more than routine maintenance. Which naturally leads to a key point in checking the mechanical assets of the car you're examining – if the car has a full service history available, the chances are it has been carefully looked after and it might well be good for a lot more miles. But this is likely to be reflected in the car body's condition, too, because if a car has been well looked after, it will have been looked after overall.

On the other hand, you may come across a car that has been well cleaned and polished, but not especially well kept mechanically. In particular, beware the 'one lady owner from new' tag, because it will rarely mean anything beneficial to you, the potential buyer. Back in the 1960s, the 'one lady owner' tag often meant that while the car had been well cared for cosmetically, it had only done short hops and so its engine temperature had rarely risen to its optimum operating level before the car was parked up and its ignition switched off. This would mean an engine running for a high proportion of its operating life with the choke applied and higher metal wear from friction. Because women are much more mobile in modern times, that problem is less likely to manifest itself now.

Even if your car's engine is 'clapped out', it's not a lost cause, for there are many mechanical components available as parts these days, either from Volvo dealers or classic car specialists. If the engine has benefited from regular oil changes and the fitment of proprietary oil filters, then the chances are that it will be in good working order, even at a fairly high mileage. But if the wrong filter has been used (the original

has a non-return valve in it), then oil can run back from the filter into the sump, with the result that when the engine is started, the bearings are momentarily starved of oil, so causing wear. You may well identify this problem by checking to see if either an original Volvo oil filter, or a reputable proprietary one, is on the engine when you examine it. You might also hear that nasty rumble when starting the engine from cold, which you the main and big end bearings are worn.

There seems to have been a period in which the camshaft on the B20 engine was inclined to wear more rapidly than you might expect. Whatever the cause, whether it was soft material from which the camshaft was made, or an oil supply problem, is open to question. But if you have a worn camshaft to contend with, you'll know it, because at around half-engine speed, you will hear a knocking reminiscent of a worn-out big-end bearing. If you have a worn camshaft, you will be very wise to replace it soon, because if it fails, or worse, breaks, then you could have four cylinders full of valve bits and broken pistons and it's not a pretty sight. Modern replacement camshafts seem not, so far at least, to suffer from the problem of excessive wear and so a car posessing a replacement camshaft is unlikely to give a problem.

Bosch fuel-injection systems are usually very efficient, although you can't avoid the fact that injectors do eventually give up the ghost and cause engines to run erratically and use excess fuel. If you want to take a chance on using a second-hand pumps or injectors, then there are plenty of 140 series cars in breakers' yards, but really it's better to buy either reconditioned units from specialists or new ones. The thermostat can fail and leave the engine running cold, too, resulting in an increase in fuel consumption, which may or may not be a

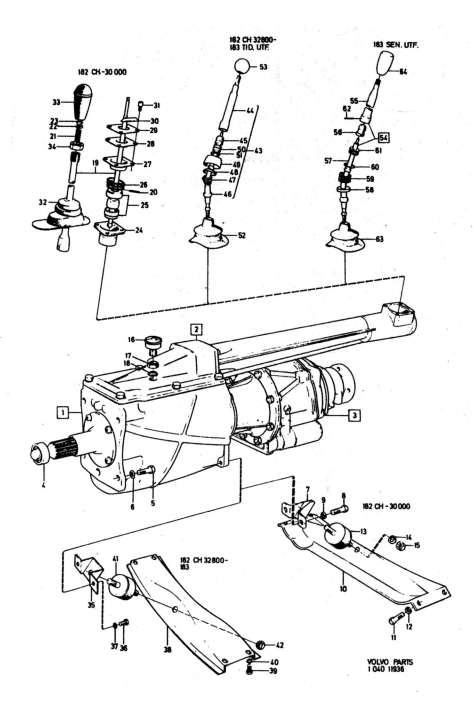

*A general view of the gearbox assembly, with each of the change
levers appropriate to the different periods in the production
life of the 1800.*

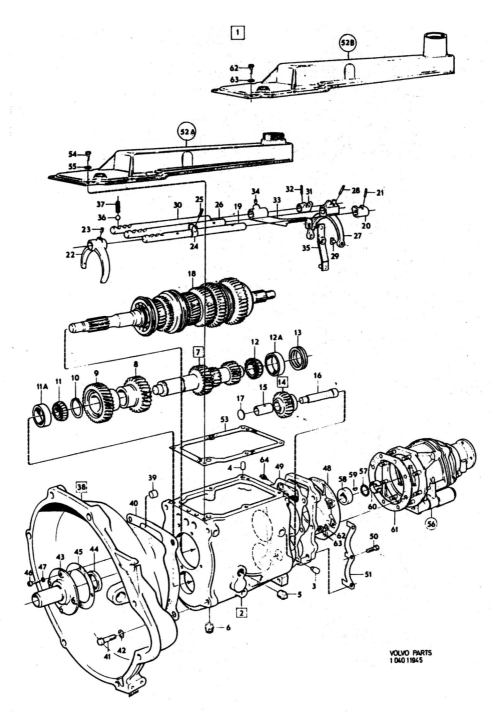

VOLVO PARTS
1 040 11945

*Looking inside, you can again see that the Volvo gearbox was made
of a tough set of components, requiring not too much maintenance.*

further consequence of 'shot' injectors. Common sense says check the thermostat before deciding you need to replace the injectors, because you might just be able to reduce the consumption to normal with a new thermostat.

Volvo gearboxes rarely give trouble, even when they have been abused with poor changes or infrequent oil checks. Generally, the worst result of infrequent maintenance is that the car will slip out of gear or you get bearing whine. But a gearbox that has had its oil topped up regularly is not often going to be a problem. Check the overdrive, however, because it may be badly worn if it has been abused. It used to be that drivers with Laycock electrically actuated overdrive units were recommended to change by flicking the switch in or out and just lifting the throttle foot to allow the overdrive to engage. In more recent times, drivers were advised to dip the clutch pedal in both engagement and disengagement, so as to minimize wear or damage risk. However, the timing of the Volvo 1800 series overdrive option came in the wake of that earlier operating practice, so the risk of abuse, in that sense, is certainly present. Look for a smooth overdrive operation before buying your 1800. And before you leave the gearbox, check the mountings; they could be cracked.

HYDRAULICS AND RUNNING GEAR

The clutch is more likely to give the odd problem. One problem, of course, could be slip because of oil on the clutch. That's normally associated with a leaking rear main bearing oil seal in the engine, which is actually not common in Volvo engines, although it does occasionally happen. If it isn't slipping, but isn't withdrawing clean-ly, check the hydraulics. The master cylinder is not likely to be a problem, but slave cylinders do leak and a set of seals will probably cure the fault. The other aspect of hydraulics that needs checking is the braking system. Leaks can be cured, but need to be indentified. If replacement is necessary, the early Girling servos and discs are no longer available off the shelf, although conversion to another type is not especially difficult.

Suspension and steering need to be carefully checked, because in a car that is not regularly used, components often seize up or suffer from surface rust. For example, brake discs can rust and when reused will pit and score, so reducing efficiency. Check the upper wishbone bushes for wear, then the ball joints for the lower wishbones. The ball joints are replaceable from proprietary sources, but on early cars these have a high wear rate, needing to be replaced every couple of years or so. At the rear, it seems to be a common fault with the 1800 that the springs will sag in time and need replacing. But there is a lower-cost, short-term remedy and that is to buy and fit a pair of Aeon rubber suspension dampers. These are cone-shaped rubbers which sit between the axle and the car's underbody and limit the travel of worn springs, so deferring the awful day. It's not an ideal solution, though, and coil springs do not cost that much.

The rear axle seldom gives problems of any kind, as it is a very robust piece of engineering, which is as well really, since replacements would be very difficult to find. As long as you ensure that it has sufficient oil, then there is unlikely to be any irritating whining from that location. Spicer halfshafts are a bit truck-like and so it is almost unheard of for one to break. What can break in that area is the trailing arms that locate the rear axle on pre-1966

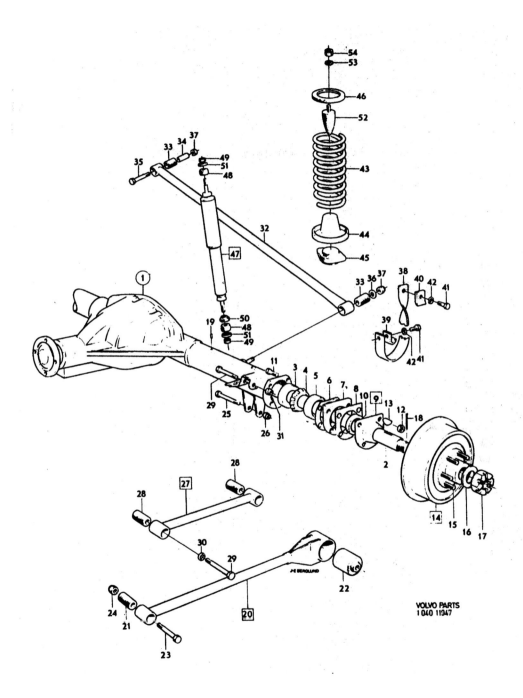

The rear axle was a similar story to most Volvo mechanicals –
if it was looked after, it gave very little trouble.

*Mike Gilbert owned this car and when he set about its restoration,
it had all the hallmarks of a well-used 1800, including the effects
of 'metal mouse'.*

cars. These are dual pressings fabricated to form a hollow section unit which collects water and, of course, rusts away in time. The later cars had a more durable rod to do the same job, but the early arms are obtainable from specialists. Incidentally, if you want to remove the rear hubs, you will need a special puller. You can remove them without one, but the risk of damage is quite high and the cost of replacements a good deterrent.

Steering parts are pretty easy to replace in the early cars and second-hand boxes can be found, although they are adjustable. But on the 'E' and 'ES' cars, the steering box is a ZF, which is no longer available new, is like hens' teeth second-hand, and, if worn, then you face a potentially expensive

problem and one which, because of the difficulty of finding replacements, will take the car off the road for a time. Now, if you're just buying the car, you will most probably want it off the road for a time anyway, but why face that kind of problem if it can be avoided? Swivel joints are easy enough to check and, even if they are worn, as they most likely will be, there are replacement kits available. The one part of the steering area of the car that you really do have to take particular care to check, though, is the chassis leg to which the steering box is attached. On many a sound-looking car, this component can be almost rusted through and if it is, it can have disastrous consequences. Quite often, on the post there will be a film of oil, from a leaky engine and steering gearbox, and it just might be okay as a consequence, but if you do not take much notice of anything else in your prospective purchase, then you need to take notice of this, for, quite literally, your life could depend on it.

RESTORING AND ENJOYING YOUR 1800

Before you even consider restoring any 1800, remember you have a choice in the kind of car you buy, based on the kind of price you can afford. It is not the purpose of this book to act as any kind of price guide in the buying of a car, but it is worth observing that, as long as you are careful in the buying process, and seek a little expert advice, then the more you pay, the better the car you should get for your money. On the assumption that you can afford a price at the higher end of prices being quoted in the classic magazines (assuming that they are anywhere near reasonably accurate, of course), then you have a decision to make based upon the question of whether you can spare the time, and want to spare that time, to restore a car. If you do, then you buy a car at the lower end of the spectrum, accepting that you'll have to some work to do, or pay for it to be done, before you can enjoy your car to the full. If not, then your alternative is to go out and buy either a sound original car, of which there are very few left, or buy a restored example.

Buying a restored example can be tricky, whether you buy it privately or from a dealer. You're back here to the point made earlier about joining a Volvo club, partly to find out more about the car for yourself and partly to find out where those worth buying are located. You then would be well advised to link up with someone who can give you sound

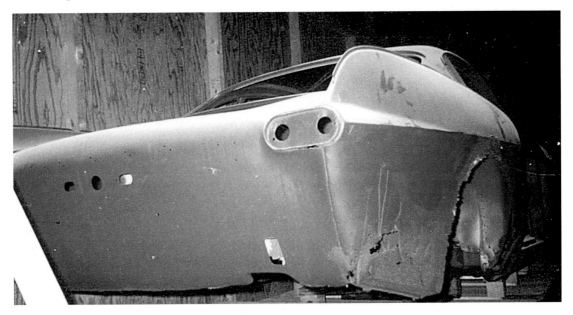

The wheel arches of Mike's 1800 were also past their best when he started work on it.

181

As the welding-up progressed, Mike's car began to come back together again.

And here's the bodyshell almost ready for paint, with many parts repaired or replaced.

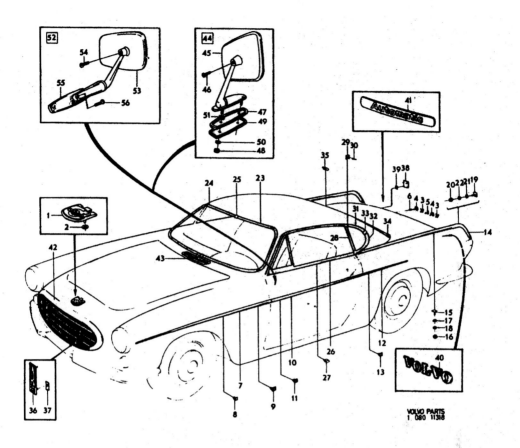

Here's the detail of the trim for the Volvo 1800 coupé...

advice on a prospective purchase – then go and look for your car. Assuming that you are successful in locating the car of your dreams, do take note of the comments that have gone before in this book during the checking-out process. Your expert colleague will certainly be of value here, especially if you buy a restored car from a private individual. If you buy one from a dealer, you should still be diligent, but at least you would have some recourse under the law if the car were to prove not to be what it was represented to be.

We have run through a pretty comprehensive catalogue of potential problems with the Volvo 1800 and you might be forgiven for wondering whether this should be the car for you. But at the end of the day, you should be aware that if you were to go looking for any of quite a long list of other classics, you would quickly realize that many of them have their problems too. What is more, many of the problems which arise with so many other makes of cars are every bit as serious or frivolous. Just about all were 'rotboxes', as already noted and all have their sensitivities. But for good or ill,

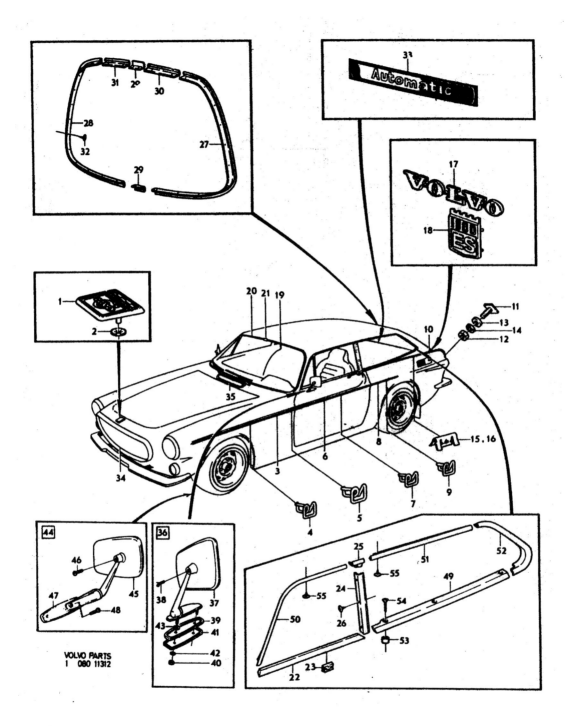

...and here for the 1800ES.

The location of the plates for the type and engine designations etc. is shown in the illustration below

1   Designation plate   1.4 Special model
1.1 Type designation   2   Engine designation
1.2 Colour code   3   Gearbox
1.3 Upholstery comb   4   Type and chassis no.

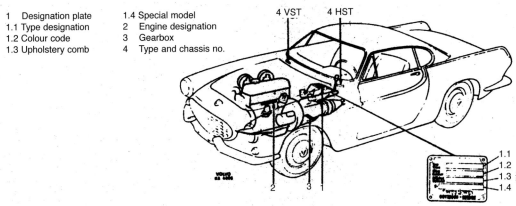

*This picture, which appears at the beginning of the parts book,
shows you where the various identifying tags are on the car,
to help you when you try to source parts.*

you've chosen a Volvo. The most likely reason you've chosen it is because of the reputation the car developed as a grand tourer. Maybe it won't handle like a Lotus, but it has long legs and truly is an excellent grand tourer, with an engine that will run almost for ever.

Looking at your own restoration, there are specialists around now who can make your life a great deal easier as you progress. It has to be said that those specialists are rarely franchised Volvo dealers, but that does not mean that their expertise is in any way diminished. Quite often, you will have to buy second-hand parts to replace defunct parts, but equally often, you'll find that you can buy newly manufactured 'pattern' parts – parts, that is, made to the original design and specification, but not by the original manufacturer. This has to be acceptable on the basis that few car makers guarantee to provide spare parts for discontinued models beyond a decade ater their demise – unless, that is, parts happen to stay on the shelves beyond that decade. And many manufactur-

ers then find erstwhile model specialists to whom they can sell their obsolescent parts inventories.

You might also want to use the expertise of a selected specialist to do part of the work of your restoration. For example, you might want the engine sorted out or rebuilt by an expert, or the gearbox, or the overdrive. You almost certainly will want expert help, unless you're absolutely familiar with the process yourself, with metal repair in the bodywork. Some panels are now available in pattern parts and some, like rear wheel arch kits, are part components intended to be welded in to tidy up the edges of the wheel apertures in the rear wings (fenders). Then, of course, the car will have to be painted. The vast majority of surviving 1800s are Swedish-built, so synthetic paint is what you're dealing with and most modern paintshops are much more familiar with synthetics than cellulose. However, the West Bromwich-built cars were all painted with cellulose and unless you're going to

185

remove all the paint down to the metal (and there's some merit in that, just to know how much metal you really have left in your car), then you'll have to use cellulose for your new paint job.

When that car is all together and ready for the road, you'll want to enjoy it and you may well want to show it off. What better place than at a club event? To do that, of course, you have to join a club and I strongly recommend you do exactly that, not just for showing off the car, but for keeping it on the road on the most economical terms. Through a club, you'll get hints and tips for best running, lower cost insurance, often parts you could not obtain by any other means and a host of new friends. So why not take heed of what many a road tester has said about the toughness, handling and sheer fun of the Volvo 1800 and go out there and enjoy it? After all, that's why you bought it, isn't it? And do not mollycoddle the car, it was not built for that.

Appendix
Volvo 1800 Models Chassis Numbers and Production Data

Model Series	Year	Body Type	First Chassis No.	Last Chassis No.	Made In
P1800 A–C Series	1961–63	coupé	0001	6000	Scotland/England
P1800 C Series	1963	coupé	6001	8000	Scotland/Sweden
1800S D Series	1963–64	coupé	8001	12499	Scotland/Sweden
1800S E Series	1964–65	coupé	12500	16499	Scotland/Sweden
1800S F Series	1965–66	coupé	16500	20999	Scotland/Sweden
1800S M Series	1966–1967	coupé	21000	25499	Scotland/Sweden
1800S P Series	1967–68	coupé	25500	28299	Scotland/Sweden
1800S S Series	1968–69	coupé	28300	30000	Scotland/Sweden
1800E T Series	1969–1970	coupé	30001	32799	Sweden
1800E U Series	1970–71	coupé	32800	37549	Sweden
1800E W Series	1971–72	coupé	37550	39414	Sweden
1800ES W Series	1971–72	sportswagon	0001	3069	Sweden
1800ES Y Series	1972–73	sportswagon	3070	8077	Sweden

Bibliography

As you would expect, a great deal of research material has had to be found for the preparation of this book. A great deal of material came from the various Volvo organizations, but much more had to be sought out from various publications. The list of material and publications given here is aimed at providing the reader/enthusiast with more material on the 1800 series of cars. Some, but notably not all, was used in the research for this book:

- Volvo brochures 1950–73.
- Various documents from AB Volvo.
- Service and Parts manuals published by AB Volvo.

- *The Volvo 1800 Gold Portfolio* (Brooklands Books).
- *Road & Track on Volvo 1957–1974* (Brooklands Books).
- *Forty Years of Selling Volvo* (Brooklands Books).
- Various issues of *Autocar and Motor*.
- Various issues of *Road and Track*.
- Various issues of *Sports Car Graphic*.
- Various issues of *Car & Driver*.
- *Volvo – Gothenburg, Sweden* by Christer Olsson and Henrik Moberger.

Material sourced from Pook's Motor Books, Leicester.

Index